Best
ü3

July 2009

A ROOM IN THE TOWN

Excursions in the Adelphi Hotel 1968

Anne Heald

authorHOUSE®

AuthorHouse™ UK Ltd.
500 Avebury Boulevard
Central Milton Keynes, MK9 2BE
www.authorhouse.co.uk
Phone: 08001974150

First published by AuthorHouse 6/3/2009

ISBN: 978-1-4389-7616-7 (sc)

This book is printed on acid-free paper.

Disclaimer

I am not I
I thou are not
Or she are not they?

Evelyn Waugh

They are not long, the days of wine and roses

Ernest Dowson (1867-1900)

To Rose and Emily

and in loving memory
of Olwen Davies

Acknowledgements

This book is affectionately dedicated to the Adelphi Hotel and all the staff who worked there. Special thanks to Maureen Harrison and Jeanette Radcliffe, bookkeeper and receptionist respectively, who read the initial drafts and many thanks to Margaret Shaw, who very kindly helped with the formatting of the book.

CONTENTS

PROLOGUE
Strange Lodgings

I

I read the advertisement in The Liverpool Echo.

It said, 'Vacancy: Bookkeeper/Receptionist, The Adelphi Hotel, single female for living-in position'. I had not expected to be living away from home, but I decided to go ahead and apply for the job just the same.

The Adelphi Hotel was legendary. It occupied a prime position in the hub of the town. Its central location put it on the map. The front of this imposing hotel overlooked the department stores and shopping area, the business and commercial centre of the city, and it looked toward the River Mersey and the docks, which up until the 1960s had provided much of the source of Liverpool's wealth. Another advantage was the vastness of the hotel which spanned 'The Block' and went around Brownlow Hill, Ranelagh Place, Copperas Hill, with Hawke Street at the back.

The hotel had six storeys and a mezzanine floor. It was built roughly in a sort of capital A shape. The top of the A represented the front of the hotel, which had a very beautiful façade and a balcony with six pillars in a Neo Grecian style of architecture. The windows were particularly beautiful, set in Portland stone and decoratively carved. The triangle in the middle of the A was known as 'the well' and was reserved for those that liked the peace and quiet of an inside room, away from the noise and busy sounds of the city.

Inside the feet of the A at the back of the hotel was the tradesman's entrance where all the deliveries were made. Here a high wall and tall gates made the hotel even more inaccessible with the wall going around the periphery of the building. At the side, near the back was the Adelphi garage. The car jockey, or in some cases, a chauffeur, would drive the vehicles around into the garage where the attendant would provide a car valet service.

Further down was the banqueting entrance and close to this the timekeeper's entrance, which most of the staff used. All those paid weekly and – the casuals, as they were called – would clock in as they came into work and clock off when they left. The timekeeper knew all the staff, and everyone knew Sammy the timekeeper.

The main entrance of the hotel was very grand. It had a private road called Ranelagh Place running across the front. The porch had a marble floor, windows with ornamental bronze detail as you might see on a ship, and doors in the same style at either end, then more steps leading up to huge revolving doors that took you to the inside of the hotel and the foyer. Outside the hotel on the street, if you craned your head, or if you were upstairs on a double-decker bus going past, it was sometimes possible to catch a glimpse into this very different world.

Inside, the Adelphi was even more impressive and spectacular. It was breathtakingly beautiful and epitomised luxurious living both in the way it was designed and the exquisite way it was furnished. The superb accommodation afforded only the very best that money could buy.

Going there for my interview I caught my breath and felt a surge of excitement, because from the first moment I set foot over the threshold I knew it was where I wanted to be. The Adelphi was a world apart from anything I had ever known. It was other people's world; it attracted millionaires, royalty, aristocracy, the Mecca of society. In its heyday and beyond, the hotel was regarded as the best outside of London. It was in a league of its own.

II

My interview at the Adelphi was at four o'clock on a glorious, warm, and sunny afternoon. It was the last week in May. There had been a few decent spring-like days, though the evenings were still cool, so I wore my new and beautifully soft beige suede coat. It was three-quarter length and felt like chamois leather. A lightweight coat, it had no collar and met with a concealed fastener at the top and then in the middle.

Underneath, I wore a suit that had a straight skirt to the knee and a short box jacket. I finished off the outfit with a decorative chiffon scarf and a pair of low-heeled sling back shoes. I walked confidently into the hotel, and I was immediately captivated.

The normally revolving front door had been stopped and was open, allowing shafts of yellow sunshine and fresh air to flood into the foyer. The reception manager directed me to sit down on a nearby rattan chair, which was placed against a marble pillar facing the reception desk. I felt comfortable waiting, and gradually I became totally absorbed in the hotel surroundings. I watched staff going about their business. It seemed to be a quiet time of day, even in an elite city hotel. Then a lounge waiter came noiselessly down the steps leading from the lounge where people sat quietly talking and taking afternoon tea.

The waiter was wearing a perfectly clean, white cotton jacket, like a steward's with a high collar buttoned from the neck right down the front. He carried a tea tray full of cups and saucers, teapot, sugar basin and milk jug, the lot; all were white china with a maroon detail. These were confidently balanced on his upturned hand at shoulder level, and he deposited it swiftly and expertly on the reception desk like he had done this all his life. He probably had.

'Here's the tea, girls,' said the sandy-haired waiter, and I could hear murmurings of approval. Someone called out, 'Thank you, Mr Harris,' as the tea tray was whisked away behind the keyboard out of sight.

The keyboard was a great wooden partition rather like a room divider with about 500 numbered pigeonholes where the hotel keys were put. The room keys were all kept on tan coloured key rings that gave the appearance of leather. They were the same size, almost, as the long metal keys and the number of the room was imprinted on the key ring, which had three points cut into it made by the locksmith.

The front desk was made of Italian marble that matched much of the décor, and there were several black telephones at either end of the desk. They all started to ring at once. Listening, I gleaned one of the telephones was a house phone. Amongst the wires I noticed a letterbox, which was cut into the marble top. The keys were posted there as guests left the premises. They made quite a din and rattled considerably as they were retrieved by the receptionists and put in the corresponding pigeonhole on the keyboard, ready for collection as and when the guests returned.

In the middle of the board at eye level I noticed there was a bigger compartment, a shelf for packages and post. On it there was a Who's Who. It also served as a look-out for those receptionists working behind the keyboard, maybe sorting the mail or doing the room allocations, so they could keep an eye on the front desk.

I watched the reception staff and visualized myself working there. They seemed competent, efficient. Fascinated, I sat immersed in these activities and goings-on when another sound not unlike a typewriter started up. It was coming from a telex machine near the bookkeeper's side of the office. A message was coming through fast and furiously, and a heap of paper was being churned out. Whatever it was seemed to cause a great deal of interest and prompted laughter. A young blonde receptionist with thick curly hair who was wearing a black velvet Alice band and a pair of pearl earrings, sat down at the telex machine and began to operate it. I noticed she wore a pearl ring in a gold setting on her finger as well. She was still laughing.

They were enjoying themselves. Then the lift pinged and some American tourists got out and walked over to reception. These overseas visitors dominated the hotel during the summer months, and nouveau riche Americans arrived in coach loads as part of Thomas Cook's Grand Tours. You could see the coaches on the drive.

Now I could hear their rather loud American drawl as they spoke in their unmodulated tones all over the front office: 'Well now, hunny, how inarresting, isn't it wunnerful?' or 'Gee, its swell here, but I don't unnerstand,' (the money), and 'don't these liddle page boys look cute in their uniforms?' These Americans came to the desk and chattered somewhat relentlessly about all the sights they had taken in during that day.

All foreign visitors had to complete a pink form, which was called an alien form, as they checked into the hotel. The American tourists travelled all over the country on their Thomas Cook's tour taking in England, Scotland, Ireland, and Wales. England would usually include Stratford upon Avon, home of the Bard and full of English history and tradition; they liked this of course. London was a must, the capital city, but in Liverpool we did not do too badly, and the Americans and Europeans liked the Adelphi with its high standard of living, its restful accommodation, and pleasant facilities. The hotel had been part of our Liverpool heritage since Liverpudlians could remember.

My gaze turned away from the reception desk at this point and focused across the foyer on the little page boys whom the Americans had mentioned. They were standing by the lounge staircase. They stood very still indeed with straight backs, hands at their sides, white gloves tucked into their epaulets, and faces to the front. They knew that the head hall porter, who was standing behind his desk, was keeping a close eye on them, and so they didn't flinch or move a muscle. How young they looked.

A cleaner went quietly about her business, wiping the bronze handrail on the staircase and polishing the marble steps at the same time. Then someone came to fetch me. I stood up cautiously and was taken into a nearby office.

It was my turn to be interviewed by the staff manager.

III

The staff manager was a fairly young chap from Northern Ireland. He had very big hands and was altogether rather large and a bit on the heavy side, but this was compensated by his gentle Irish drawl and easy manner. He was smartly turned out in carefully pressed morning suit, and highly polished leather shoes. His thinning brown hair was neatly combed back. I noticed he wore a wedding ring; it looked new.

My interview began reasonably well. I was genuinely not nervous; after all, I was on home ground in Liverpool. After the initial pleasantries and some references to my application, which mentioned I was a bookkeeper with an accountant, I vaguely remember being asked how good I was at maths.

'I'm good at adding up and handling money,' I replied.

'Just what we want,' said the staff manager, and he made notes while I elaborated. I had practised for this interview and had tried to anticipate the type of questions that might come up, and so it all went pretty smoothly and uneventfully. Then, as if to fill me in, the manager went on to tell me something about the history of the place and the staff who worked there.

The manager explained how this truly magnificent hotel was owned by the British Transport Hotels group. A railway hotel, it was situated near the main line railway station, Liverpool Lime Street. He said the company owned more than thirty hotels in all. The head office was at St Pancras Chambers, London.

The Adelphi provided employment for a very large number of people and had an enormous payroll. Part of the attraction lay in the range of jobs it offered and the security it gave. The hotel provided regular work, career opportunities, accommodation, and a sense of family for a lot of Liverpool folk, many of whom lived in the town by the Bullring, or in nearby Everton and the Dingle. Other employees lived on local branch lines, those that had not been axed, and were entitled to free rail passes to and from work. There were also opportunities to move to other parts of the country by transferring to another hotel in the company. There was a lot of scope.

Many of the female staff came from Ireland and had living-in positions in the hotel where they spent their entire working lives. When staff got too old or infirm to go on, the manager would personally find a suitable Catholic nursing home or retirement place for them where they would be cared for, as they had been cocooned and institutionalised in the hotel.

Continental staff striving to make a career came to work in the hotel; a real cosmopolitan atmosphere prevailed with gallant young French waiters, attractive Italians, and swarthy Spaniards. There were a few lively Liverpudlian waiters thrown in as well; many tongues were spoken at the hotel. It was global. On one single shift I learnt there might be a dozen or more foreign waiters working in the French restaurant.

Many of the staff worked really long hours for small wages; but it was a good living to have: they got first class experience and training in a prominent hotel, they were able to learn English, and the rail concessions made travel within reach.

The hotel was indeed a refuge; a safe haven with plenty of company and a chance to make friends. There was always a hot meal to be enjoyed at the end of the working day. It was an anchor and a home, and so the Adelphi held onto many things from the past, including its staff, of which there were many old retainers. The company kept them on;

nobody got 'finished- up'. I discovered all this during the course of my interview. It was a revelation.

The staff manager thought it important for me to know as much as possible about the organisation; especially about the front office and reception. The reception manager was called Mr Constantino. He was a handsome Portuguese fellow who looked every bit the part: a flamboyant character, he ran reception with aplomb, efficiency, and style. He was the last word in sophistication. Everything about his appearance was perfection. His voice with its strong Portuguese accent would resonate from reception, and his hand would strike firmly on the bell to summon the page boys, their hats at an angle and the buttons on their jackets gleaming as they came running to the desk.

Mr Constantino knew everyone and had a certain panache, which made him seem exceptional; guests were made to feel special and were warmly welcomed. He was a very well known reception manager. When he left the hotel for a new position his replacement was a younger man, a tall blond German fellow who was quite subdued if not dour. He was lacklustre and uncharismatic. Maybe the job was not what he expected. It was very demanding, consuming. He did not stay long.

After that Miss Olwen Davies was appointed head receptionist. She brought the glamour and youthfulness that was needed back to reception. The desk was once again lit-up with a vibrant and sparkling atmosphere. Olwen was striking and had stunning good looks, brown eyes that could dance, and she radiated charm as she greeted guests. She sounded frightfully English, was very elegant, and had a laugh that was infectious and could be heard across the foyer. Olwen had worked on reception, as a shift leader, at the Adelphi for a several years. She knew the job well. Her title later changed to reception manager; it proved to be her metier and she stayed for another twenty or more years after that, while other staff came and went.

Meanwhile, I listened intently to the staff manager who was telling me there was a big turnover with the assistant managers. This was mainly because they moved around to different hotels in the company. They lived in and had many different roles and responsibilities, including banqueting, sales, and marketing management. Those who were married might have a property in the suburbs, but their families would stay at the hotel during the weekend when they were on duty.

The managers worked alongside the hotel staff turning their hand to everything and anything and carried bleeps so they could be contacted at any time of the day or night.

There were also a number of young trainee managers, all male. Those who were single almost invariably ended up falling in love and marrying someone from any one of the numerous departments in the hotel. It was an occupational hazard. At the weekends, though, they would relax, let their hair down, and use the penthouse suite on the sixth floor.

The general manager lived permanently in the hotel with his wife, two teenage children, and dog. It was their home. The family had a wide circle of friends who were often in the public eye: well known television, film, or theatre personalities. They would stay regularly as guests.

I could tell as my interview progressed that I would have a lot to live up to as the company was not only looking to recruit new staff, but wanted those who possessed that something extra, a star quality. I was just thinking I would have to try a bit harder when a golden opportunity presented itself:

I heard the staff manager ask if I had any questions. He sat back in his chair, smiling benignly, his fingertips touching together.

I thought for a few moments before speaking. 'Why yes.' There was so much I wanted know. I inquired about the special business. Then as an afterthought added, 'Can you tell me something of the functions and the residents too?'

The manager gave me a good insight into the hotel. It was the place that wealthy businessmen chose to stay. There were tycoons and international businessmen with an eye on commerce and trade. Shipping companies and import and export offices in the city employed large numbers of staff and the container docks were about to be built out at Seaforth.

The Bank of England was situated at 22 Castle Street not far from the Town Hall, and the governor of the Bank of England visited the Liverpool branch regularly. He came from the head office in London and stayed at the hotel, usually accompanied by his wife. Their names were on the hotel VIP list. The manager showed me the VIP list and the special business list, which had a bulldog clip holding lots of papers together on a clipboard. I skimmed it and noticed Ford Motor Company mentioned.

The Ford Motor Company had opened a new factory at Halewood earlier in the sixties, and a group of their top German people, maybe five or six management consultants from the company, became permanent residents. They flew into Speke Airport where they could reach both the motor car plant and the hotel easily. They came to Liverpool every week, going home at weekends, and the Adelphi was familiar and welcoming. Others lived in the hotel for months or maybe years and the same rooms were let each week. These residents came to depend on the hotel staff and it became their home away from home.

One lady who made the Adelphi her home was a Miss Coulthard. She had lived in China most of her life and had painted much of the blue and white bone china that we see today in the shops, the willow pattern plate designs. Each pattern and design tells a story. She was a very interesting person. Miss Coulthard was tiny, thin, and ancient. She ate like a bird. She wore a loose, silky, long grey coat most of the time and a large brimmed hat that resembled a native hat; perhaps it was one. Her silver hair would be pulled back off her face to make a bun on the nape of her neck. She was very genteel and refined.

Strangely enough, though, this elegant lady would sit outside on the Adelphi steps in the summer sunshine, maybe on a tranquil Sunday afternoon, and bask in the sunlight, enjoying the warmth. It was unheard of and considered rather common to sit on the front steps, in full view. But no one minded, and the hall porters looked after Miss Coulthard. They made sure she had a pot of tea as she sat there watching the world go by.

IV

The staff manager went on at length about some things that I already knew. He spoke about the pop artists, groups, and singer-songwriters who came to Britain, mostly from America, to play at the showcase Sunday concerts held at the Liverpool Empire Theatre close by in Lime Street. The Royal Court Theatre entertained the ballet and opera companies. I remembered the Liverpool Playhouse in Williamson Square was refurbished in 1966 with a bigger stage and dressing rooms. The glass tower was built to accommodate a new entrance, booking office for the theatre and also a restaurant named the Redgrave Room, which was soon to be opened by Sir Michael Redgrave, his wife Rachel Kempson and The Redgrave Family. Little did I realise, sitting there in 1968 that I would get to meet these great people of the theatre.

The Adelphi was the place the Redgraves came to stay. It was uplifting and wonderful working there, meeting this wealth of culture, especially at a time when the theatres were enjoying a renaissance.

The Everyman Theatre was staging great new plays and productions. Actors and artisans would flock to the city to work with the repertory companies because they were the best. Many would use the hotel as their base. Many films were made using Liverpool as a backdrop.

The film of Neville Smith's book *Gumshoe* was shot in the hotel. A room was used to double as Room 327, the Plaza Hotel with George Silver playing the 'Sydney Greenstreet' type character from '*The Maltese Falcon*'. Mr Silver came down in the lift to the hotel lobby wearing only a pair of very brief trunks. Albert Finney played Eddie Ginley, the bingo caller in the working men's club, and Billie Whitelaw played Ellen. Most of film stars on the set were residents in the hotel. Nev Smith gave the staff on reception signed copies of his book.

On such occasions somebody always threw a party. This was a time when many modern day artists and celebrities laid the foundation of their careers in Liverpool.

The manager spoke highly of the Philharmonic Hall. The guest musicians who played there would stay in the hotel where they liked to relax in between their busy and demanding schedules. It was exciting hearing their impromptu rehearsals, he said. Nearby, Rodney Street was the Harley Street of London. Nicholas Monsarrat, the writer, was born in number eleven, and he would dine at the Adelphi when visiting the city in later life. All these areas in the city brought eminent people into the hotel.

At a later date, the Adelphi became home to the Liverpool Press Club, which took over part of the basement near the cellars. Behind the green baize door many well known journalists from all the main newspapers would frequent the bar. They came to Liverpool covering the big football matches and to file copy on the many important stories in the great maritime city.

Several grammar schools in the town brought a youthful population to the area, and the sound of children's laughter and voices could be heard as they circulated around town. In one of the new comprehensive schools, Dr Eric Midwinter was setting up projects and new initiatives to help teachers in the inner city. He based himself at the hotel.

St George's Hall along Lime Street was home of the law courts, and the Adelphi ran the 'bar mess' and the annual Law Society dinners. This meant a great many learned friends patronised the hotel. If a cab was needed, the porter or car jockey used a whistle to call one from the taxi rank on the corner of Copperas Hill. Frequently guests needed to reach either the Liverpool Football Club at Anfield or the Everton Football Club at Goodison Park. Harold Wilson sometimes required a cab to visit his constituency in Huyton. In those days, Harold Wilson was in his first office as Prime Minister (1964–70). He would check into the hotel, pipe in hand and wearing his familiar Gannex Macintosh. He stayed at the Adelphi regularly, with his wife, Mary, and his secretary, Marcia, and would hold his press conferences in the hotel. Mary gave a copy of her poetry book to reception.

The Grand National out at Aintree Race Course brought many rich and famous people to Liverpool, film stars and royalty alike, plus a large contingency of Irish race goers. It was not just the racing that attracted them but the hotel, which was held in high esteem. The Grand National was always a momentous occasion for the Adelphi and for the people of Liverpool. They would mill into town, down the hill, from these various Liverpool locations walking, driving, or using the buses going past the place in which many people felt a civic pride, the Adelphi Hotel.

The hotel was a world where there was very much a sense of tradition. To many people employed there, the Adelphi was the bedrock of their society where generations of family had worked and passed through over the years; a rite of passage. Age and background it seemed did not matter. Certainly for many of the staff it must have retained something of the old days; even if it was pure nostalgia and wishful thinking.

V

We moved on to conditions of employment. The staff manager explained that front office staff were entitled to alternate weekends off; wages were £6-4-6d per week plus 12/6d service charge. Pay day was fortnightly on Thursdays. This wage included accommodation and food – full board, in fact – and a free rail pass home. Other perks of the job included more rail travel concessions: five free rail tickets anywhere abroad per year and a rail pass that entitled you to purchase any number of rail tickets for a quarter of the fare.

The bookkeepers and receptionists in the front office were known as 'the black staff'. All the female staff who worked in the front of house had to wear black dresses with long sleeves, and this uniform was not provided by the company. Accommodation for female staff was at the back of the fifth floor, where no men were allowed. It was known as 'the convent.'

These were the rules and all I remembered of the interview. Then we stood up and walked out of his office, and he took me into the foyer. I glanced about excitedly. He was going to show me around.

We were standing at the cashiers' desk. This was next to reception and had a pillar dividing the departments. There was a blue counter which held seven drawers (one for each bookkeeper) and above it a florescent sign saying *cashier*. 'There you are,' mused the staff manager, 'your name is in lights'. In the centre of the office were two massive desks. Then on a sort of podium was the head bookkeeper's writing desk, complete with a traditional brass desk lamp and a swivel chair. I spotted a large cast iron safe on the floor and turning round I saw lots more safety deposit boxes behind the door. Opposite there was a window that looked out into the town.

Near the front office were three telephone boxes, each with a house phone and an outside line. The telephonists operated the switchboard from the mezzanine floor near the control room. When a call came through to reception for a resident, staff would first check if the key was lodged there before paging the guest, who might be dining in the restaurant, relaxing in the lounge, or maybe having a drink in the American Bar.

On several occasions Margot Fonteyn was paged to take telephone calls from her husband Roberto 'Tito' Arias in Panama. It was often a bad line and they would have to shout to be heard. Margot would leave the phone box door open as it got hot and airless. She was so lovely, serene, and charming, just like you would imagine a prima ballerina to be. Her husband resumed his political career in 1967. Margot Fonteyn subsequently retired from dancing in 1970 and went to live with him in Panama.

Next to the telephone boxes was the ladies' powder room and cloakroom, which was staffed. Mounted on the wall nearby were a couple of brightly lit showcases with elegant jewellery displays. Next to these were two Otis elevators for hotel guests and a few stairs that took you down to the breakfast room, which was signposted. The paintwork in these public areas was subtle and the finish on the paint gave a lustrous appearance. It combined well with all the decorative brass and metal work found throughout the hotel: on the lifts, staircases, doorways, and on the mirrors.

The main staircase in the centre of the foyer went up to the lounge. This had a bronze handrail and more ornamental decorative bronze work that was the replicated many times throughout the building. Up in the lounge, which was vast and high-ceilinged, there were marble pillars tinged with pink. French doors opened out into the French Restaurant on the right hand side. The Sefton Grill was on the left; more French doors. It was all very symmetrical. The floor was carpeted and clusters of small tables and groups of armchairs were strategically placed so they could be seen from the lounge pantry.

The surrounding area of the lounge floor was marble. Several times during the course of the evening the duty bookkeepers would walk around the periphery of the lounge to collect the bills from the two restaurants. They would pass through the hypostyle, which was behind the French doors at the back of the lounge. The hypostyle was an enormous area resembling a gallery. It had four massive iconic pillars reaching up to the ceiling, supporting it. The staircase in the lounge divided and continued to the mezzanine where it evolved into a great main staircase which led to all the floors.

VI

The hotel cuisine was superb. The Sefton Grill specialised in English food. The maitre d' in the restaurant was always full of bonhomie. He ran the restaurant like a tight ship, as indeed it was a replica of the smoking room on the Titanic. His elderly cashier in the restaurant had been part of the hotel since time immemorial; nobody seemed to want to retire. I had been told staff loved their life at the hotel and they just kept plodding on until they pegged out. There were no risk assessments in those days, and health and safety issues were largely common sense.

When I was working there you could hear the cashier rustle as she padded along, making her way through the foyer, long after the Grill had closed for the night. In one hand there would be an envelope with the money and the banking sheet, and in the other her large black cloth bag, which she would swing by its round handles until she got to the front office. Trembling slightly, she would put the takings in one of the little safety deposit boxes that were kept there behind the door.

The French restaurant, too, was indeed very special and beautiful. It was the only one of its kind around. There was much to admire:

not least the walls, which were inlaid with lovely wooden panelling, the lighting, the tall mirrored doors, the secluded alcoves, and the arrangement of the tables. The maitre d' in the French wore black tie and tails and cut an impressive figure while paying attention to the needs of his dinner guests. The two female cashiers who worked there were sisters, and another cashier worked in the French wine office. There was a resident pianist who played gentle arrangements on the beautiful grand piano. He had such a natural flair. He could play anything. The music made the atmosphere in the French restaurant seem even more inviting, more romantic.

Decades before, in 1922, Henry Hall had joined the Railway Group as resident pianist. He later became musical director for the hotels. He would broadcast from Gleneagles, but during the winter months when there was no golfing and the hotel was closed, he would transfer to the Adelphi. Many of the staff and indeed many of the older generation of Liverpool people remembered Henry Hall and the wonderful tea dances that were held in the immense Adelphi lounge.

There was still a sense of Englishness there, lingering about the lounge, where quintessentially English afternoon teas were served. These always began with the tiniest, triangular, bite-size cucumber sandwiches and the welcoming pot of tea with a selection of delicate cakes and dainty pastries. The lounge was where guests could quietly sit and do their own thing: read, rest, or take refreshments, waited-on by highly experienced and knowledgeable staff.

The staircase on the right in the foyer took you down to the couriers' room, the still room, and through to the kitchens and basement. In the basement there was a swimming pool, though in 1968 it was devoid of water. Nevertheless, it did resemble a Roman bath in its design and the way it was tiled.

The staff manager continued his brief tour and pointed out the baggage lift and luggage room. Behind the mirrored doors he showed me strong room where the big safe was housed. To the other side of these mirrored doors the cloakroom and newspaper stand could be found, and an elderly porter called Pat looked after these. He sold the London *Evening Standard,* which was highly popular, The New York *Herald Tribune, Le Monde,* and the *Financial Times.* Any newspaper could be obtained from Pat, who worked from behind a small counter, watching as events unfolded in the front hall of the hotel.

Then there was the American Bar.

VII

The American Bar was a central part of the hotel and was situated in the very far corner of the hotel foyer, unobtrusive yet exclusive. It had the now familiar sparkling mirrored doors, and inside the windows overlooked both the front of the hotel and Brownlow Hill at the side. The bar ran lengthways, and behind the counter were mirrors and glass shelves for the optics and bottles. Everything gleamed and shone, and the glasses were polished until they dazzled. The bartenders, like the restaurant staff, wore white cotton gloves to keep the glasses pristine and finger mark free. The bartender, a young man called Brian, wore a grey jacket with a bow tie, while the head barman wore a maroon jacket.

The most famous head barman in the latter half of the twentieth century was Albert Dwerryhouse, a real gentleman, well known for his knowledge of cocktails, his equanimity, and charming personality. He had a prodigious memory for clients' names and could remember both the name and favourite drink of customers, even after years between visits to the hotel. The American Bar was a favourite haunt for many.

The porters stand was in a prominent position by the front door of the hotel. The tall and congenial head hall porter, Harry H, had worked in the hotel since he was a boy. Standing erect behind his podium, he beheld all the public activity that was going on in the hotel foyer. There was always much activity. Harry was charm itself, with a majestic manner and well modulated voice. He was articulate. His telephone was situated next to the revolving door, and a separate door at the side was used to bring in the luggage. The hall porters (which included the night porters) were a large staff. They worked very closely with all the departments but especially with reception. There was also a youthful car –jockey who was smiley, shy, and quietly spoken. He looked happy in his job.

Five or six page boys worked in the hotel under the direction of the hall porters. They were taught how to do things properly; how to behave, how to stand, and how to address guests. They were disciplined and quietly taught their job by the head hall porter: 'Don't do things this way but that!' said Harry. And having instructed them on these finer points, the hall porter would propel them into action. Sometimes they were admonished if they failed, but not often. Indeed, many of the page boys went on to become hall porters themselves and stayed many years, sometimes all their lives. We knew all their names by heart. Robert and Geoffrey were two of the nineteen sixty-eighters.

Opposite the porter's baggage door was another side entrance with a stone staircase that took you down below to the basement, and the barber's shop. It was a quick way into the hotel for black staff going through the basement to the baggage lift and up to the fifth floor.

Standing at the front door of the Adelphi, underneath the clock and by the hall porter's desk, you could get a good view of life outside the hotel, better still if you went on the roof. From the rooftop you felt on top of the world. It felt good to get some fresh air there and feel the salty breeze. If the wind was blowing in the right direction it was possible to hear the ships sirens and the tug boats on the River Mersey. Everyday there was the one o'clock gun fired from Birkenhead, by which you could set your watch.

Walking out of the hotel and pausing for a moment on the steps, I looked around at the familiar scene. Already I was seeing it with new vision. The Adelphi gave one a sense of belonging and a part of being in the Liverpool landscape. I felt there was so much to learn and discover.

I moved forward to merge with the bowler hat brigade wending their way home from offices and places of work, and together we made our way to the railway station.

VIII

My letter of confirmation dropped through the letterbox a few days later. It was now official. I had got the job subject to a satisfactory medical examination at Rail House. I had to report for duty a week or so later, arriving at the hotel by teatime on the Sunday, where I would ask for the duty manager and the housekeeper, who would take me to my room.

Shopping for my dress was easy. It was an eye catching little black number from Nanette's, a well known dress shop at the top of Bold Street, and was a crepe material beautifully made with a gored skirt. Next to buy was a pair of black patent leather court shoes with a high heel, and to finish off the outfit a small, black beaded handbag. On my list of things I needed to buy was an alarm clock.

So happily laden down with my goods, I met my sister Margaret and together we headed for lunch at the Mariners Restaurant in Lord Street to celebrate my not-so-run-of-the-mill job and even more exciting, strange new lodgings, in the town.

CHAPTER ONE
Fifth Floor Convent

I

The fifth floor 'back' was strictly for single women staff only. This designated living accommodation was generally known as the fifth floor convent and was situated at the back of the hotel, where women staff had their own rooms. No men were allowed to visit or be entertained on these premises, hence the title. It was a sackable offence, so these ground rules were generally kept.

For some female staff, the hotel had been their life. They were married to the institution, but a woman marrying in the real world meant a duplication of role, and she was required to leave the company. That is what happened. So, there we were, in residential accommodation on the fifth floor: a single sex, a body of women, a female society ensconced in the hotel where everyone knew each other. Sometimes people would congregate in each other's rooms to swap stories and talk. It was companionship. It was certainly an education mingling with such a cross section of society, wandering about in such a great space on the fifth floor.

There were twelve young bookkeepers and receptionists living there, plus the female heads of departments and seconds. These positions in such a grand hotel held a certain cachet. They were among the few jobs available for educated women that didn't restrict you to a nine-to-five office culture and a dull repetitive routine. The hotel generally attracted young types who were eager to travel, and those who were fluent in languages. It enticed young women dreaming of marriage, because the male guests who stayed in the hotel were for some a catch.

As well as the bookkeepers and receptionists living on the fifth floor back there were chambermaids and housekeepers. Life was relatively simple and straightforward with few demands. It was refined and leisurely. We were a hotel family, a mixture of young, middle-aged, and elderly women who came from different backgrounds and walks of life, all with different aspirations and going separate ways.

These female quarters had two wings with a long corridor running across joining them (the crossbar of the A) and doors at either end, which made it more secluded. The night lights in the corridors were left on all the time, giving a dim glow. Mostly it was tranquil. We lived enveloped in a secure and safe stillness. There were no worries, and we could wander around as we pleased; in our quilted housecoats and indoor shoes, without wearing make-up, in our night attire, using the telephone, listening to music, drinking coffee. It was a girl's world.

At each end of the two wings, near the bottom of the corridors, were two large television rooms. These sitting rooms had lots and lots of armchairs and settees, although people didn't loll about much; there wasn't time. The chambermaids, housekeepers, and occasionally the receptionists used to sit there some evenings, often too tired to do anything else except flick through a magazine or two and maybe watch a couple of programmes before turning in for the night. An elderly Irish chambermaid who was titchy tiny and spoke ever so softly could be found there, nodding off quietly. She liked watching the Eurovision Song Contest, which was a must every year not least because Ireland always had competitive entries.

Sunday was a markedly quieter day upstairs on the fifth floor. It was a day of rest in more ways than one, and many staff would have gone home for the weekend. Those remaining in the hotel made the most of the serenity in readiness for the fray on Mondays. Living-in staff went to church. Those belonging to the Church of England would attend the parish church of Liverpool, St Nicholas, situated close to the pier head in Chapel Street, not far from the Town Hall. Roman Catholics worshipped at 'Paddy's Wigwam', as the Metropolitan Cathedral was affectionately called because it was built in the round and had a lantern tower that coloured the inside of the cathedral in lovely hues. It was consecrated in 1967. Then there was the Synagogue and the Mosque. The Synagogue was a grade one listed building and the first outside London. The Mosque, the first one in Great Britain, was situated at 8 Brougham Terrace.

It was on such a peaceful Sunday afternoon that a small number of people gathered silently downstairs in the hotel foyer before being met by the manager and taken to hear a will being read. It was Brian Epstein's, who had been The Beatles manager.

II

On the fifth floor our bedrooms were mostly double accommodation with some singles. All had fitted carpets, central heating, washbasins, twin beds, and they were cleaned on a daily basis by the chambermaids. There were two bathrooms to every couple of bedrooms. These were quite something and were set back off the corridor sort of art deco style. They had large glass panels or openings which had small panes of glass. Then both on the left and right hand side of these there were a couple of steps up and doors into the bathrooms. They had deep roll-top baths and large washbasins, good lighting, mirrors, and lots of space to dress and do your hair. They were always kept thoroughly clean and well heated with decent floors and big windows.

Further along was the ironing room. When the uniforms changed from black dresses to woollen worsted, tailored suits in British Rail blue worn with white cotton blouses; the ironing room resembled something on the lines of a Chinese laundry; washing was everywhere. There were lines and lines of wet blouses hanging everywhere to drip –dry. Ironing boards and irons were left out as they were continually in use.

Then there were the wet tights. The change from stockings to pantyhose started to take place in the mid to late 1960s. Of course, before this ballerinas had been wearing tights, and you could purchase thick, patterned winter tights. But with the advent of the miniskirt, a dazzling and exciting new mode of dress, we hitched our skirts up as high as they could go right up to the tops of our legs, and tights became a 'must have'. Stockings and suspender belts for everyday use were discarded. Aristoc and Wolford (with its easy identifiable black stripes on the packaging) were two leading brand names, but the real improvement had come with Dupont and the invention of Lycra, which gave elasticity and stretch to the tights; no more wrinkles around one's ankles or stockings falling down. Ladies underwear had become high fashion, sexy even, and changed completely for the better. Nobody wanted to be dated or outdone.

The chambermaids had their own uniform. They wore a long, royal blue nylon overall which had a kind of geometrical pattern in a slightly darker blue. Those chambermaids responsible for the fifth floor cleaned the staff quarters at the back as well. It was good returning after work to find your room had been aired, vacuumed, beds made, wastepaper bin emptied, wash basin cleaned, indeed everything done.

The two electricians would change the light bulbs, check electrical fittings, sockets, and plugs. The night fireman, Fred, complete in uniform, came along the corridors every night to check the sand and fire buckets and the alarms and fire extinguishers. You could recognise his heavy footsteps. Occasionally, one would catch sight of the floor waiters delivering room service. Otherwise there was no sign of anything male about the fifth floor back.

At each end of the corridor were black wall-mounted telephones; on lifting the receiver the switchboard would connect you to internal numbers in the hotel or get an outside line. Any early morning calls were put in with the night telephonist Ted, and he in turn would pass these on to the night porter's desk. The telephonists all lived out but would take their meals in the stewards' room where they talked non-stop, relating stories from the switchboard room. These were always amusing and kept everyone riveted. One telephonist was a Liverpool girl who had once been a nun. She was very saintly although she could talk for England and wouldn't stop to draw breath, a Liverpool trait maybe. The second head was Canadian with a great telephone voice and manner. Then there was a Scottish lady who was full of witty repartee and made us laugh. Another telephonist came from over the water, across the River Mersey, and for a time her young daughter worked as a bookkeeper. The head telephonist ate separately in the couriers' room. The telephonists all knew their jobs inside out, and they knew all about the hotel guests.

The stewards' room where we ate was in the basement off the kitchens, in the same area as the laundry, staff games room, and staff bar, not far from the timekeeper's office. There was a back lift in the kitchens manned by an elderly gentleman called George. Next to it was a stone staircase to the floors, which was useful as an alternative. There was a more modern service lift that was used predominately by the floor waiters for room service. Sometimes staff living on the fifth floor back would use the floor service amenities on the sixth floor, if only to make hot drinks and leave tea trays, which in turn would be put in the dumb waiter and sent back to the kitchen. There was a dumb waiter in the French wine office. This went right down to the cellars and was how the bottles of wine were brought up.

III

The head bookkeeper in those days was Miss Wilson. It was a prestigious position. Miss Wilson had worked in the hotel since she was a girl, and now she was getting on a bit. She knew more about the Adelphi than anyone. Her single room was situated at one end of the fifth floor corridor.

Miss Wilson had the remains of good looks and wore her short, light brown hair in tight curls all over her head as was the fashion of the time. Her mouth was painted with bright red lipstick drawn in a cupid's bow, and sometimes she overdid the rouge just a tiny bit. She wore a black two piece; the jacket rested on her generous hips and it would be loosely tied with a corded belt. A brooch would be elegantly pinned on the lapel of the jacket which had one, or maybe two shiny jet buttons, though these were never fastened. Her eyes were bright and observant; she was quick to notice things. She had good business acumen.

In her youth Miss Wilson was quite a dynamic lady, and rumour had it that she had once owned a motor bike. She spoke 'quayte naycly' in a matter-of-fact sort of way, and her voice would carry as she had a habit of chuntering as she moved efficiently round the office. She had high standards. It was her way to fuss. Getting older and letting go of the reins was hard, seeing changes and standards drop: so very many staff must have passed through the front office, under her regime. Some stayed for years while others drifted in and out, five minute wonders. But Miss Wilson, or Willy as she was fondly called, was of the old school, a relic from the past, and she was very much the boss when on duty in the front office. She laid down the law and gave her orders.

As I arrived to take up my new position she was nearing retirement at the end of a long working life. She must have been tired. The job was hard with the endless conventions and societies, the influx of hotel guests with their endless complaints and problems, the tedious duties and repetitive tasks. But we still had to learn her ways, her method of doing things. And she would harp on: 'Would somebody please see to that gentleman at the desk?' She would say it crisply without looking up from the banking. 'Now, thank you!' Then she would peer sternly, with raised eyebrows, in your direction and prattle on, tutting very loudly until someone moved. We kept our heads down otherwise engaged, totalling up figures or counting the endless varieties of foreign currency and travellers' cheques; oblivious to everything, even the smooth velvet voice of the film star James Mason, who was giving yet another Oscar winning performance, playing to his audience, us, as he waited to settle his account. We never batted an eyelid.

Miss Wilson was very much the boss; she who must be obeyed. She had an air of authority and was inflexible on most matters, but when in Rome *et cetera* one had to do as the Romans, and even little things mattered a lot. Perfume, for example, was not to be worn in the morning. It was a cardinal sin, so we had to leave our Norman Hartnell In Love, Carven Ma Griffe and Hermes Caleche behind… The rituals of scent had to be discarded. No one dreamt of doing otherwise. Only on Tuesdays, which she took as her rest day, could we relax and let our hair down a bit. Sindy would sit on her chair and swizzle round and round being high spirited and impish. There was no one around to chastise, no one to say it was inappropriate behaviour. 'Freedom!' we shouted, albeit short lived.

Mornings in the front office, with Miss Wilson at the helm, were always frantic with big check outs. The hotel bills were split with the top paper copy receipted and given to the guest on payment of account. The carbon copy underneath detailing method of payment would be initialled by the bookkeeper and filed away. Once the morning rush was over and all the London trains departed from Lime Street, the front hall went very quiet.

We closed down the business, and the machines would be locked and a final reading taken. The till rolls would be removed from the cash register machine and the dates changed. Then we would try and balance. Control would arrive to take the inside of the desk drawer with its many compartments and the day's business transactions upstairs to their office to check and audit.

If we couldn't balance the books that was another matter, and we had to do 'call overs' and search until we found our mistakes and rectified them. Sometimes the glamorous people over on reception would pick up if things were not going so well on our side of the office. They would hear us agonising over mistakes followed by the debates, post mortems, and blow-by-blow accounts, trying to sort the mess out. Olwen would watch and give Jeanette a knowing look and say, 'Here we go, these bookkeepers, hopeless cases, haven't balanced again!' And they would laugh in good humour at our downcast faces as we reckoned up.

The blue hotel bills were passed over from reception with the tariff, the room number, and name of guest. Sometimes if they had a forwarding address they went to the ledger clerk, a delightful middle-aged Irish lady called Miss Kelly, after they had been included in the daily balance. Yet another tray held the laundry accounts. The hotel laundry service was used by local professional people and the Irish boats.

There were always three or four tin trays full of hotel accounts. They were filed in green cardboard covers and started at the first floor, then onward until the sixth floor. Many of these rooms were suites or stockrooms; then there were singles, doubles, twin beds, fly beds, en suite, and so on.

On Sunday afternoons when the hotel business was slow and there was a let up in the proceedings, I would teach Miss Wilson how to play chess during tea breaks and show her the moves and the rudiments of the game. She in turn would explain the company regulations and show me the way the office operated; she loathed the fact that the hotel wasn't what it had been. No, it certainly wasn't what she had been accustomed to, and she disapproved. On a day-to-day basis things appeared to stay the same, but looking back, when Miss Wilson tried to remember the past and how things were done in the hotel, then the changes became noticeable.

IV

Upstairs on the fifth floor back, at the opposite end of the long corridor from Miss Wilson's room, lived Miss Davies, reception shift leader. We were always called by our proper titles in those days, no first names. This room was a rectangular shape; the furniture shone and the tops had clear surfaces. Everything was kept in its place. No junk.

It had a bright, sunny aspect and was a room with view. Out of the window directly opposite you could see Lewis's department store, best known for its nude statue, officially entitled Liverpool Resurgent but rechristened 'Dickie Lewis'. It became a well known meeting place. Jacob Epstein designed the sculpture and Pete McGovern wrote about it in his song, 'In My Liverpool Home' which was immortalised by the Liverpool Spinners. This area was perpetually thronged with shoppers and business people coming into the town or going out via Central Station with its low level trains running to Chester and Wirral.

Olwen liked her room and had many personal belongings dotted about. Actually they were rather carefully arranged, lots of bits and pieces including a set of red leather suitcases that she kept on top of the wardrobe, a twenty-first birthday present given some years earlier and which she used on her weekends off. Then a tall, wide necked, crystal vase, another twenty-first birthday gift. Her room was always full of fragrant, freshly cut flowers usually bought from Elsie Bruce the florist or from Fishlocks. Sometimes they would come from an ardent admirer or as a thank you from a company.

In the cabinet there would always be a bottle of Tio Pepe or Dry Sack sherry and chocolates or sweets in a dish on her coffee table. Lots of photographs in frames were on show, treasured pictures of family and friends. There would be a neat pile of glossy magazines and periodicals. Library books, too, were featured prominently in the room as Olwen, like most of us, would use the lending library at the Bluecoat Chambers in nearby School Lane.

When Miss Davies was appointed reception manager she moved down to the fourth floor. Here the room had a lobby, which made it more private as well as soundproof, and it had fixed mirrors everywhere, which gave the illusion of space and light. Originally the Adelphi rooms had been furnished by Waring and Gillow and Maples, but Olwen made some changes and invested in several larger items of furniture: armchairs with matching footstools, china, cut glass wine glasses, and a music centre, amongst other things, and her room gradually took on her persona and reflected her taste. It was hugely comfortable.

Once or even twice a week she would have her hair washed and set by John over at Andre Bernard's Hairdressers. She rarely washed it herself. She loved shopping and bought her clothes largely from Jaeger and Burberry.

We found it hard to guess exactly how old Olwen was as her birth date was like Easter, a movable feast. It didn't much matter, but we were sometimes curious as to how old she was and would have a book on it.

V

There were lots of us women milling around on the fifth floor, and we often took afternoon tea together. This was between four and five o'clock in the stewards' room and consisted of tea and fresh, thinly cut bread and butter. The bread had been made earlier in the day in the hotel bakery. The smells coming from the bakery of the warm dough being mixed were delicious: the crusty cobs, soft barm cakes, golden loaves dusted down with flour and gently baking in the ovens were mouth watering, but very tempting to those watching their waistlines.

The stewards' room was always friendly, and there was always a pot of tea on the go with someone to pour out a fresh cup and bring it over to you while you sat down, and rested your weary feet. The kitchen area had red tiles on the floor and there were large sinks and draining boards, stainless steel units and tops with hot plates. There were no windows as it was in the basement of the building, so there were always lights switched on.

Cissie was in charge. She was scrupulously clean, salt of the earth and married to the kitchen clerk Arthur. Bella also worked there; she was so old, like Methuselah. She had plump arms and was so small, round, and fat she could hardly walk. Her head would bob about. But old age was venerated in the hotel and she was a welcome addition to the work force. Maisie, who worked with them, was much younger, but her large brood of children gave her face a careworn look. Would they ever know how hard their poor mother worked to feed and clothe them? Then there was Mrs Onions. This was pronounced almost phonetically, Oh ny on s. We never questioned the reasoning behind it. She was older too and had shiny black hair set in waves like the River Mersey. Blonde Betty came later.

The staff uniforms were long, white cotton wrap-around overalls, and hair was worn tidily off their faces. They were all locals, honest folk who took an interest in everybody and everything. The square dining table where the girls congregated to eat was covered in a large white linen cloth. We used the corners of the tablecloth as napkins. There we would sit in the warmth of the stewards' room, elbows on the table, talking. The big, brown, Bakelite radio would be switched on quietly in the kitchen until Sindy arrived and fiddled with the frequencies to change the radio station. When she found some music on Radio One she would grab hold of Cissie and dance her around the kitchen.

At six thirty in the evening supper was served. This would usually be a hot meal, maybe haddock and poached egg. When working on late duty, around nine or ten o'clock in the evening, chef would send a silver salver, (or silver flats as they were sometimes called), full of daintily cut sandwiches filled with all sorts of tasty morsels and garnished with a selection of nuts, crisps, and salads up to the front desk. If chef was in good humour and they were not run off their feet in the kitchens there might be prawns with a Marie Rose sauce, which nearly everyone liked, especially Maureen. She would make a special trip to the kitchens to ask chef nicely if we could have them.

The staff bar and games room was popular amongst the hotel staff. Staff could go there to have a drink and a break, or play pool, or play on one of the fruit machines. A bookkeeper went there daily, as soon as the sun was over the yard arm, for a Jameson whiskey. People had their reasons, and nobody judged. Rose ran the staff bar, and she deposited the takings in the cashier's office with the rest of the hotel banking every night before catching the last bus home.

VI

As a staff we were very much influenced by any cultural events taking place in Liverpool, because the hotel was in the thick of it. We were 'in the know'. Many brilliant, gifted, and famous artists appeared in Liverpool, and as hotel residents they would generously give complementary tickets to the staff. We felt honoured. If there was a book from a play, a novel, or a soundtrack from a film, maybe an LP, this would be bought as soon as pay day arrived.

Taste in popular culture varied. The younger members of the staff would frequent the Liverpool hot spots; everyone had their favourite haunts. They might eat out, maybe at the Shakespeare Theatre, which had recently been refurbished. It was where Sam Wannamaker had been director and later artistic director in the 1950s. There was a so much choice and such a selection of places to go.

If we were tired and needed to get away from the confines of the hotel there was always the cinema along the road, which showed popular films of the day that required little or no effort to watch. Just to fall asleep lulled by the warmth and stillness in the picture house was bliss.

This was a bygone age, yet it remains so vivid and real. We crammed so much into life and eased through the years in a sort of parallel universe unaware of time passing.

CHAPTER TWO
The Bed Sitting Room

I

Lucinda and I shared room 550. We had always been best friends, kindred spirits one might say. We had grown up and ambled through school together, and now we were going to work alongside each other, Lucinda as a receptionist on the same shift as Olwen and Patsy. Mr Constantino was the reception manager at the time.

Lucinda had needed somewhere to live because her parents were moving away from Liverpool. Full of bright ideas, I had piped up that maybe she should come and work at the Adelphi Hotel with me. There was a vacancy coming up for a receptionist because one of the girls, Eleanor, was leaving to get married.

'You would have somewhere to stay and I am sure you would like the job. Do apply,' I implored. It certainly sounded feasible and would solve her problems.

Listening, she looked at me and nodded thoughtfully, considering her options. She made the decision. It happened just like that; it was a real stroke of luck or maybe it was fate. All the girls shared rooms and it was usual to put receptionists and bookkeepers together so they would work the same shifts. Lucinda walked into the job and was put with me in room 550.

It was pleasant enough, a large inside room with twin beds, south facing and overlooking the well. All the Adelphi rooms had slight differences in their views. Our view from the window was of the triangle. There was nothing much to see, only the main stairwell across the way, and we could sometimes hear the faint echo of distant kitchen noises drifting upward. If you leaned out of the window it was possible to see the glass roof far below that covered part of the middle area.

Our bedroom was spacious, the door strong and sturdy. It was highly polished with a sheen, classic Adelphi, with gleaming brass handles; all the doors were made like that, though some on the lower floors opened outward into the corridor like on the liners, but our door opened inward in the usual way. The room had a tall ceiling, as did all the hotel rooms, and I thought it was just lovely, so huge, airy, and light.

The beds were Staples beds and quite high. The mattresses were deep and well sprung, heavenly to snuggle into at night. In the far corner of the room there was a large washbasin with a towel rail, mirror, and glass shelving for toiletries. Next to that was the window.

The window seemed to be a focal point and was framed by the room. It had lots of small panes of glass and a deep windowsill. There was a white voile curtain, which all the Adelphi windows had, and it would billow when the window was opened. There was always some sort of breeze blowing in off the river.

The furniture in the room consisted of twin beds, two medium-sized armchairs with casters so they could be moved around easily, a low wooden coffee table, two wardrobes with long mirrors, and two dressing tables that also had mirrors. The fitted carpet was patterned with a sort of mottled design. There was, of course, central heating, so it was very warm, but because it was an inside room, in the middle, it was like toast.

Outside our room the wide, shadowy corridors seemed endless. They were lengthy and had identical doors and exits leading to different places in the hotel, and it all looked very similar at first. It was very quiet and austere. The room next door to ours was furnished as the housekeeper's office, which was open for business during the day but was generally closed in the evenings.

Next to that was Sindy and Patsy's room. They were both recent arrivals like me. Sindy was the youngest of us at seventeen, and she still had some adolescent traits which were endearing. She was a bookkeeper. Patsy, a receptionist, hailed from Manchester and retained a strong regional accent of which she seemed proud; she made no attempt to hide it. Most of the front office staff spoke in Received Pronunciation with clipped accents like the Queen. Off duty, Patsy and Sindy would often hang out together in the hotel and could be found singing or shrieking with laughter and joking, or merely playing music in their room, which they decorated with posters. Sindy and Patsy were happy, outgoing souls who liked company and were good neighbours. Their room was more like a den where people would converge, and they would leave their door ajar when they were about.

On the left hand side of 550 were the bathrooms, always two together, and then more bathrooms opposite, all in the same art deco style. Lucinda and I felt these were almost en suite and exclusively for our use. These bathrooms, which were set back off the corridor behind large glass panels, were bright, roomy, and full of natural light.

The voile curtain could be used as a screen if needed. Lucinda and I used the bathrooms as dressing rooms and to do our toilette. The white baths were deep and the water felt buoyant. There were large chrome taps, and plugs that were round and bigger than a tennis ball. We had endless hot water, enough to draw a full bath. To lie back and soak wallowing in the bath water was sheer luxury.

II

I was satisfied and happy. I really liked my job in the hotel, was content in room 550, and felt a sense of freedom because there was nothing to do. It was a domestic calm, but Lucinda did not feel the same. She was disappointed with the place. In a way the situation was a stopgap for her, a stepping stone, but already she felt institutionalised in the hotel.

'Look, Anne,' she would say, sighing despondently as she tried desperately to explain. 'This room is just… oh it's just… so ordinary and mundane. Everything is monogrammed with BTH (British Transport Hotels) embroidered on it, so drab. I'm bored stiff with it. It's fully furnished and therefore doesn't reflect who we are. It says nothing about us or our personalities.'

Lucinda had these notions and a keen sense of individuality. She wanted to give the room an identity and introduce the concept of home, somewhere we could relax.

'Well it's not quite as bad as it seems,' I replied earnestly, because I really wanted Lucinda to settle in and like it. 'We could try and put our stamp on it, give it an image and make it different, make it ours. I know we'll revamp it.'

And we did just that. We went to great pains to turn the hotel room into a pad, a sanctuary, our place.

Lucinda was definitely a more practical person, an independent spirit and a regular girl guide, who thought we should reorganise things properly to make it into a bed sitting room. We had similar tastes and ideas and busied ourselves making changes, classifying and putting things into piles to keep or put away. We wrote lists of things we needed to buy.

It was like moving day. Looking around the room, we began to push the furniture side to side, up and down, into the middle. We heaved it around this way and that. Then we upended the mattresses and repositioned the beds so they were both on the same wall as the door, facing the window. The bedside table with the alarm clock and lamp was put in between the beds, and we put our bedtime reading there.

We shared a dressing table, but we had a large wardrobe each, not that we had a huge amount of clothes. Lucinda liked colours and fabrics like linen and fitted clothes with wide, bright, leather belts or waspies, while I liked muted tones, kaftans, reefer jackets, long scarves, and shoes with wedges. We didn't move the wardrobes in the event.

Making a sleeping area had been easy and already the room was taking shape and looking better. A lot better. We kept going, stopping only for tea. We redesigned the opposite side of the room, putting the armchairs at an angle with the coffee table in the middle with our magazines on top. The other dressing table served as a sideboard, and we used it for photographs and potted plants or flowers when we could afford them. This was near the window, and this area became our sitting room.

Lucinda, always a very generous and kind person was now brimming full of new ideas. She dashed off into town and bought lots of household items for the room all out of her own pin money. We had every luxury. These items included various objet d'art and included a pretty, bright orange and red cotton lampshade with a frill round it, like a mop cap. We used it for the main light, and it brought colour into the room. Surprisingly it hung directly above our coffee table in the centre of the sitting room. Everything we were surrounded with gave us pleasure.

Lucinda also purchased a green sisal fruit bowl which she filled with fruit and nuts. We stood the bowl on the sideboard, on top of a Welsh tapestry runner with some other bits. We had some vivid scatter cushions, a kettle, radio, and a record player, but we used the hotel trays, silver flats, teapots, and coffee pots, which everyone did, though we used our own coffee mugs as they were bigger and held more.

We enjoyed our mugs of hot, frothy milk, which we got from behind the swing doors in the lounge pantry after we finished work at midnight.

III

Still not completely thrilled, we had a rethink. Lucinda was busy. She was preoccupied, organising a pile of Penguin paperback books in a corner of our sitting room and doing various other arrangements, paying attention to detail, as usual, when she asked, 'What more can we do, Anne? It's still not enough.' She said it carelessly shrugging her shoulders, looking at me hopefully and for inspiration. We didn't argue the point but racked our brains.

In a sudden flash of inspiration, it came to me. 'How would it look if I painted the furniture white, all of it?'

It was a toss-up whether or not to go ahead, but then we considered it essential in order to create an art nouveau atmosphere, reflective, luminous, light; a white room. We aimed for minimalism and a more contemporary modern look.

I bought two large pots of white gloss paint and proceeded to paint the two double wardrobes; a big job and only possible by climbing first on the armchair and then the dressing table. Some of the paint was applied too thickly and was rather uneven; you could see the brush strokes. Like a moiré I thought, deluding myself, but never mind. It would dry.

Stepping down, I painted the dressing table and the sideboard, two coats. 'Not bad.' I looked around with smug satisfaction to see if there was anything I might have missed. Oh yes, the coffee table.

We never sought to ask permission and just went ahead slapping the white paint on the beautiful solid wood furniture. The white paint certainly gave a new dimension to the room.

I had some brightly coloured Mary Quant motifs bought on a shopping spree in London. These green, pink, and red (typical Quant) multicoloured floral patterns were placed underneath the glass top of the dressing table. They looked artistic and decorative. I stood back to admire my handiwork: Fabulous.

I gave an ecstatic scream of joy. 'Umm… yes… it works, that's it! Marvellous,' then, 'Quickly Lucinda, come and look! It's all done,' I cried: 'Look at my master stroke. 'Voila!' This truly was an act of genius, and so the bed sitting room was reborn.

We were indeed full of ingenuity and thought we had been enterprising. The whole effect was atmospheric, dramatic, and different.

Lucinda and I were full of joie de vivre now. We felt quite proud of ourselves and had delusions of grandeur; just a touch. Such was the influence of living amongst an affluent society! We took to inviting friends to the hotel, to our 'Des Res' for afternoon tea, and we would sit around cup in hand as if to the manor born. The friends were keen to visit us and share- in our hotel experience but, they were more interested in seeing our interior design and the new look they had heard so much about. Lucinda and I warmed to this topic and related to them how we had planned it all.

We offered a personally conducted tour of our estate showing off the main points of interest to our guests, mainly the bed-sit, and the fifth floor corridor, including fire exits and lavatories and bathroom/ dressing rooms. We would entertain regularly and did this quite a lot, until the craze wore off or we ran out of money.

IV

Lucinda and I were also pioneers of the healthy food movement, which played a big part in our bed-sit life. We were paid fortnightly on Thursdays, and on pay day would shop in Coopers, (a high-class food store), Brookes, in Bold Street, or the Health Food Shop in Whitechapel and buy what we deemed healthy foods. We were not especially interested in the hotel cuisine because we were on a health food kick and had a mania for keeping thin.

We had our own views on what constituted proper food and thought ourselves connoisseurs. This eclectic list included: Bircher Muesli, buttermilk, bought from Lewis' Food Hall, St Ivel lactic cheese, and something called Yeastrel (which tasted like Bovril), and Mitchell Hills, 'Healthy Life Biscuits'- very crunchy, and oh yes, Beulah's rich golden honey. For dessert or snacks we ate fresh fruit, halvah, and Vitanut. In St John's Market we bought dates, stoned raisins, and nuts, especially brazil nuts, which were Lucinda's favourite.

My sister Rosemary made us peanut butter, yogurt, and sent food parcels, which near Christmas would include homemade chocolates with truffles and vermicelli. Later on her culinary skills extended to soya bean loaf and cottage cheese, but her forte, for which she was renowned, was Mrs Murphy's famous no-bake chocolate cake. This we gave to our guests. I drank cider vinegar in hot water with honey and persuaded myself to develop a liking for it. It was a fad. And we also got a taste for dandelion coffee. We never indulged in anything stronger; I suppose we were more or less teetotallers. How we enjoyed these so-called healthy gastronomic delights.

Sometimes Lucinda and I would seize the day, being young and having a zest for life, and catch the London train just to eat in Cranks Restaurant. We would enjoy a bowl of their scrumptious soup and buy some Cranks honey to bring back. Or we might take the tube to Leicester Square and the Swiss Centre to sample their delicious muesli.

How pseudo we must have seemed, pretentious moi, but we thought we were original and full of savoir faire. It was accepted by the manager that I was vegetarian, and I was allowed a jar of pure English honey from the stores because I wasn't eating very much of the hotel food.

When we were off duty Lucinda and I would go to the Liverpool Playhouse, get cheap tickets up in 'the gods' on the hard seats, and savour the productions. We had a lust for culture, a desire for knowledge, so we enrolled for night school at what we thought was a still life class at the College of Art in Hope Street, only to find out it was a life class, but no matter. We went along, armed with pencils and paper, ready to learn to draw the unexpected and perhaps unknown and making not very fluid sketches, but making friends with the students and models.

We went regularly to concerts at the Liverpool Phil, and I went to dancing and keep-fit classes. We both loved music, and Lucinda had a portable record player, so frequently the jazzy sounds of Stan Getz and Astrud Gilberto or the sound track from Claude Lelouch's film *A Man and A Woman* could be heard drifting out of our bed sitting room.

There was always a lot to talk about. Reading was a favourite pastime of ours, and we would lie about engrossed in novels. *Lord of the Rings* by Tolkien was on my list of books to read. It was our second copy of the book because the first one had been chewed by a Labrador pup called Lucy who belonged to a friend. Lucinda read other books, not trash but different ones. And she loved her glossy magazines. We read in the newspapers about the war in Vietnam and were relieved Harold Wilson kept Great Britain out of it. We supported the ban the bomb (CND) movement and tried to master a new language, Esperanto. It was a learning curve, or some would say a craze, and I practised on Lucinda, but it never came to anything.

Getting used to our bed-sit being 'the white room' and different from the other rooms on the fifth floor back was easy. We got accustomed to it. In fact we forgot all about it.

V

We forgot all about it, that is, until one day Lucinda got sick. She had all the symptoms of influenza and exclaimed how awful she felt. The two hotel doctors, who were father and son, held a surgery Tuesday and Thursday afternoons. This was in a room somewhere along the fifth floor corridor after they had eaten a good lunch in one of the hotel restaurants. We did our best to try and stay fit and healthy bearing in mind the surgery hours; we were not much inclined to go to the doctors anyway. However on this occasion, after a close examination of herself – we were both good at self diagnosis – Lucinda exclaimed that she still felt unwell.

'I think I will have to see the doctor.'

'Perhaps if you just stayed in bed and dozed a bit?' I faltered feebly.

'I don't think so, Anne,' and with that she fell back into bed with a lot of moaning and groaning. 'Oh Anne, I can't swallow. My throat is sore.' She did sound hoarse, I supposed.

'I feel so awful. It's the… lurgy,' she croaked and lay there inert.

'Lurgy,' I whispered. 'I hope I don't catch it.'

You could tell just by looking at her she had a fever. She was flushed and there were beads of perspiration on her forehead. Lucinda was indeed ill; too sick to get up, too poorly to go on duty. There was nothing for it but to summon the head housekeeper, Miss Murphy.

Miss Murphy was a small, rotund, middle-aged Irish woman who lived in a suite of rooms on the fourth floor away from us. She wore glasses, and had a hairstyle just like the Queen. In fact, she looked every bit like HRH, but here the similarity ended. She spoke much too quickly in a strong Irish brogue and was sharp, abrupt, and business-like. Always on the go, she kept on moving; she never stood still. Miss Murphy would carry a bunch of keys in her hand, which you could hear clinking as she marched brusquely along the corridors in her long-sleeved, serviceable black dress, inspecting the rooms, checking; very thorough this housekeeper; (more high standards). Miss Murphy, we had been told, had a sense of humour, but there were no sign of it today. Today was like a state visit.

I was combing my hair in the mirror when the she came knocking loudly on the bedroom door, with her knuckle on the wood. She then paused and rattled the key in the lock. As the door handle turned Lucinda's eyes met mine in the looking glass and our eyes went wide in trepidation. We knew that we were for it.

It was no ordinary, unlived in hotel bedroom that the housekeeper entered into but 'Our World'. Standing in the doorway Miss Murphy got a complete view of 550 and the new layout. She whirled around, surveying the scene and the odd, white surroundings, a sort of panoramic view. There was a queer expression on her face and she looked strange. Her entire working life had been spent in hotels, but this was something quite unexpected. She must have thought us Philistines; white paint on the Adelphi furniture, her beautiful oak and mahogany furniture. She swayed unsteadily on her feet and faltered; only for a second, and clicked her tongue.

Room 550 was definitely not at its best; anything but, and looked well below par, like Lucinda. It looked seedy with shades of a sick room: stuffy, window shut, curtains not drawn, aspirins, and wastepaper bin overflowing with used tissues, the bedclothes rumpled and dishevelled. It was a bit squalid. In short, it did not much resemble the smart piedà-terre we had once envisaged. I sat by Lucinda, who was lying down in bed, looking blotchy and unwell.

Miss Murphy was in shock. She seemed, momentarily to be at a loss for words. The silence was awful and hung in the air. She stared, her attention now solely on Lucinda, who was shivering and shaking in bed.

The housekeeper regained her composure and said, 'It is only a little cold you have, I'll send for the doctor but you will have to go home until your symptoms subside; you can't be sick here. I'll hear no more about it now, but you will do as I say.'

'And as for you,'… oh dear, she had remembered me… 'You will be up in front of the general manager if the room isn't put right and… out of this hotel, Miss. You've got until five o'clock tonight!'

It was then Miss Murphy had a fit. She flew right off the handle.

Then she left us alone: dazed.

'Well, didn't she sound cross?' murmured a pathetic little voice from somewhere buried beneath the bedclothes. 'Did she mean sacked?'

The elder hotel doctor arrived and listened to Lucinda's chest, then he asked her to put out her tongue before prescribing antibiotics. After this she beat a hasty retreat and went home to be nursed back to health. I was left to transform the White Room or else suffer the consequences.

It was pretty dismal. I was at a loss and didn't know what to do or where to begin. It was a mammoth task.

VI

I had a brainwave. It came just at the right moment. The old locksmith, Dennis, who made all the hotel keys, replacing the lost and broken ones, might be able to help me. His workshop was on the fifth floor, just along from room 550, around the corner. The locksmith was a mine of information where the hotel was concerned. He would know what to do; he was sensible and wise.

'How can I possibly get the room straight, Dennis? I can't even remember what it looked like.' I sobbed in between hysterical outpourings and wails. 'Then there's the white furniture.' I blurted out.

'Don't take on so, lass, you mustn't fret,' he replied in his soft Lancashire accent. 'It will blow over you'll see.' He pondered thoughtfully for a while; an age. I waited. This needed thinking through. I was hoping he could come up with something to save me. He sat, leaning heavily on his walking stick. I thought him seriously old. He wore navy blue overalls in the workshop because it could be very grimy work; a dirty business, making keys. Anyway, here was this kind, dear man who was sympathetic and understanding. After a while he got an idea and a plan started to take shape.

Dennis knew all the hotel staff and he telephoned round the various departments and spoke to everyone employed there: the French polisher, the valets, the joiner, electrician, porter, the sewing room ladies, and the chambermaid. He told them what had happened, and without exception they all said yes they would rally round. It wasn't a problem. They came in droves to room 550, each with their own trades and skills and crafts, to get things back to normal in the room.

The French polisher began by trying to salvage the wardrobes and dressing tables. First he stripped two coats of white gloss paint off the furniture. Everywhere looked disastrous: the room was full of debris. Things looked as if they couldn't get any worse, but they did, this was just the tip of the iceberg. Everywhere had to be washed down, scrubbed and finally vacuumed. When the room had been cleaned and the dust settled, the French polish was applied to the prepared furniture. This was a slow laborious process.

Staff toiled all afternoon. The furniture and drapes were put back in their original places; well, some of them anyway. In the nick of time they were done. The room looked more or less as I had found it, in keeping with British Transport Hotels' tradition: shipshape, comfortable, clean, and tidy accommodation. It had been a close call.

'It feels just like when I first moved in here,' I said to Dennis. 'No one would ever have suspected otherwise.' Amazingly, the furniture was restored to its former glory. The room felt familiar and in character once more. 'I don't know how to thank you all. I am most deeply grateful,' I told the staff; staff in a million with hearts of gold. I had got to know them quite well during the course of the day's trials and tribulations. I glanced around, feeling pretty fortunate. Miss Murphy took the long view, and all was forgiven and forgotten. It was never mentioned again.

I closed the door behind them. My spirits restored, I breathed a huge sigh of relief and collapsed completely exhausted onto my bed and contemplated the room; our room in the town. Stretched there on my back, hands clasped behind my head, I looked up at the ceiling and, blinking, I saw Lucinda's bright, frilly, cheerful, and most colourful lampshade staring down at me.

VII

A few weeks later I celebrated my twenty-first birthday. Alec Rose had gone round the world in his yacht. England had won the last test match in the Ashes Series at the Oval and 'Hey Jude' by The Beatles was a hit. Lucinda and I were kept busy preparing and getting ready for my big day. Party Saturday!

My sister made not one but two birthday cakes, which she iced and decorated beautifully. My mother gave me a gold wristwatch, and I bought a new dress. It was white with long sleeves, a blue ribbon around the waist, and pearl buttons down the front. The material was voile over silk. It was soft, pretty, and feminine.

I had twenty-one friends at home for cake and champagne; then we left for dinner at the Shakespeare. God was in his heaven and all seemed right with my world.

My actual birthday fell on a Monday. On duty in the Adelphi the page boys, Robert and Geoffrey, brought cards and telegrams on silver trays to the front desk throughout the day. Lucinda gave me a beautiful and expensive shiny white oilcloth umbrella; just what I wanted.

The door to 550 was left wide open for visitors. It looked chic, sophisticated, and reflected our ideals. We still had a genuine vision of how our bed-sit should look: artistic, illuminating, and full of charm, even without the special effects of white gloss paint.

CHAPTER THREE
The Time We Got Drunk On Success

I

In the October, my mother died suddenly in her sleep. We knew that she had not been feeling well, but never realised. It was a shock. I never liked the autumn much after that, the empty trees, the early morning mists, damp and darkness. It reminds me too much of those awful desolate and sad days, the beginning of life without my mother and encountering death.

When I returned to work at the hotel a week or so after the funeral it became obvious the staff were looking out for me as I learnt to cope with my bereavement and sense of loss. The hotel routines and daily rituals provided stability and reflected the family infrastructure of the hotel.

Out of the blue I was selected to represent the front office on a committee. Everyone had heard of it: the entertainments committee. It organised the prestigious and exciting staff Christmas party. It was a big event and a highlight of the hotel year for the staff and all those involved with British Transport Hotels. The evening began with a wonderful dinner, which was followed by a show; a class act.

There was a big sense of occasion, and guests were invited from far and wide. Invitations went out to those on the board of directors in head office at St Pancras Chambers; the top nobs from London, and lots of other incredibly, very important people, also from London. Everyone rubbed shoulders here. There was no distinction. Those employed in other British Transport Hotels and staff who had retired attended as guests of honour. Current employees had permission to bring a friend or family member. There was a lot at stake as the Adelphi had been the flagship in the company in the days when things were done properly; well, maybe after Gleneagles or the Midland, anyway. Each had their special charm.

The staff manager presided over the entertainments committee and welcomed any suggestions. First of all a date for the party had to be arranged.

'Can anyone remember what happened last year? We have to decide whether to go before Christmas or after Christmas?' he asked politely. Everyone deliberated. Tommy, the hall porter, seemed to know best and people listened.

Then, 'Can you organise this, that and the other?' he instructed in an amicable tone. The committee went through the copious lists of things to do with the staff manager, and gradually everything started to take shape and fall into place as if by magic. It was informal, relaxed, and fun.

Arranging the function seemed a breeze. After all, the catering side was easy and straightforward once the menu for the dinner and the wine lists had been agreed. It was what we did best. The head banqueting waiter was asked to sort out which of the extra staff would be prepared to work the evening of the dinner dance. Everybody on the entertainments committee had some kind of responsibility and job to organise. The main event, of the utmost importance and the highlight of the evening was the entertainment, the show!

There was much talk of previous years and of artists who had performed on these auspicious occasions. A short list was made of celebrities who could be approached to make a guest appearance at the dinner dance this year. Who could be invited to star; to do a spot and sing, dance, or act? This was a stumbling block because the date for the party was very close to Christmas, chosen specifically for that very reason, because it was a quiet time in the hotel. People went home for the holiday. There were not many residents, let alone famous artists staying in the hotel, no one who could be called on to help us out of this pickle. It was quite a fix we were in with no one to star in the show. We sighed and it began to weigh heavily.

Then suddenly, 'We could ask Pam', suggested someone.

II

Olwen was friendly with Pam, who had once worked on reception in the hotel. Now she lived in a flat somewhere along Gambier Terrace. In her youth, Pam had been a Bluebell Girl, a professional dancer.

Bluebell Girls had special qualities. Not only would they have had extensive ballet training, they had to possess poise and beauty and be at least five-foot eight-inches tall, if not more.....Five foot-eleven inches perhaps. They danced at the Folies Bergere in Paris.

Pam was one very tall lady with long legs that seemed to go on forever, and she still looked every bit a Bluebell Girl. Dancing had been her life, and she was still very much the dancer. She had not forgotten her rigorous training schedule and exercise regime. The staff manager telephoned her and asked if she could produce a show, choreograph it, the lot.

She said that yes, she was prepared to do it, amazingly. It would be a challenge because there wasn't much time, only a matter of weeks. The staff manager was just so relieved that Pam agreed to do the show. He was also anxious as to whether she could pull it together in such short space of time. It was not long until Christmas.

The committee heard on the bush telegraph that there were three of us in the front office, Liz, Gina, and me, who could tap dance after a fashion, and flattery induced us to reveal that yes, we had been to dancing schools and performed in theatres, so that clinched it. We were persuaded against our better judgement by the powers that be to do a star turn on the show.

The rest of the bookkeepers and receptionists in the front office were auditioned and press-ganged into participating as well. Nobody was exempt except Olwen, who was now officially the wardrobe mistress, and in charge of making the costumes, and doing alterations with the help of the sewing room ladies. It was not an easy task to make us look like professional performers when we were all different shapes and sizes.

Everyone was kept busy. The page boys were ordered about and usefully employed. They were sent on errands out of the hotel to fetch in comfort food from Mary Whitehill's chip shop up the road on Brownlow Hill. Then they would go on messages to buy cigarettes from over the road at Lewis's. Sometimes the page boys went to fetch endless pots of tea and coffee from the still room to help keep us going while we rehearsed.

III

Dancing lessons were held every Sunday afternoon with Pam in the Masonic Suite, and in a way I looked forward to these. The Masonic had a sprung wooden floor. It was like a ballroom and lovely for tap dancing. We could hear if any beats were missed in our taps, or if we weren't picking our feet up properly. Then we would run through numbers and watch ourselves in the mirrors, taking it from the top. Ann Miller, eat your heart out!

The receptionists and bookkeepers, all the girls in fact, had separate lessons and learnt different dance routines and sequences. They became the chorus line. It was pretty complicated stuff, and they were all arms and legs and quite ungainly. Seemingly nobody could remember their right from their left. Then Pam told the chorus girls they had to have hats and hold silver moons. It was all too much and there was an outcry, but Pam had no time for nonsense. Heavens above, she had a tight schedule and a reputation to keep. She was a Bluebell Girl.

Meanwhile Gina, Liz, and I got to grips with the time step, fall overs, wings; pull backs, and learnt to 'spot' all over again. It was great fun using the top corridors to pirouette, twirl, and dance along:

speeding faster and faster, down and down, as if we were on the Cresta run, and we would all be laughing and singing to the same tune.

Dancing was pretty exhausting as well as time consuming. Nothing else got done. It was only the adrenalin rush that kept us going. Rehearsals took up every single minute of the day when we were not working, but it helped me to forget my grief momentarily, although I was in a dreamlike state and saw nothing of my surroundings or people or places. I didn't notice anything very much. I felt bereft.

IV

The weeks' flew by, and in no time Christmas was upon us and the day of the show arrived. The girls were having serious misgivings now about performing, but it was far too late for a change of heart.

Panic set in as the hotel started to come alive and buzz with activity in readiness for the function. It certainly looked seasonal and festive. The florist had used Christmas decorations and greenery for the displays. A Christmas tree had already been decorated and stood on the stairs leading to the lounge and another tree, even bigger, had glistened and glittered in the banqueting hall for several weeks.

The dinner dance was being held in the banqueting hall that night, and everything from the tables and chairs to the glassware was now being set up. The stage was festooned with cables and wires, cameras, footlights, and plants, which made the event, become a reality.

As staff could invite friends to the party, Lucinda and I asked her younger sister and another girlfriend as our guests. Being hospitable types, we said of course they must stay overnight in our room. We pushed the beds together to make a double. This should have made more space, but everywhere was in a state of flux. There was a mound of stuff lying about: shoes, stockings, uniforms just left on the floor, trays of dirty coffee cups covering just about every surface and top imaginable. It was untidy, a bit upside down. Totally out of character for us, but then life had been out of sync. There was never any time for anything but our dancing classes and rehearsals for the show.

Night time arrived all too soon, and as the evening gathered momentum the dancing girls became somewhat the worse for drink, or in the words of the head bookkeeper: the demon drink. Even Lucinda had had one over the eight. They were tight. It had just dawned on them that they were going on stage and they needed a prop! It all felt a bit surreal, a bit strange.

On the fifth floor we cleaved together as we got dressed, toing and froing between each others rooms as we prepared ourselves for stardom. There was much giggling and mirth as all the dancers dressed and put on their stage makeup and costumes. The sparkly clothes covered in sequins and glitter looked breathtaking. We were done up like band boxes. Olwen had done an absolutely brilliant job. How sensational and chic we were dressed in all our finery. We looked as pretty as a picture, and had the essential component, which was glamour.

And so the mood lifted and the atmosphere took on an excitement that became infectious. It was intoxicating, and we became more delirious as the witching hour approached. The thought of dancing on stage in front of such a large and distinguished audience was so very thrilling. We were on a high, a roll, and unknowingly we adopted the persona of theatricals and became luvvies.

Crammed together in the service lift going down to the function we felt quietly confident, or perhaps it was an attack of first-night nerves. No one spoke as we entered into the world of show business. You could have heard a pin drop.

V

The banqueting hall looked fantastic and was pulsating. It was packed, and the dinner was almost finished. It seemed everyone had enjoyed a tip-top meal, the drinks were still flowing, and people were leisurely reclining. There was a sense of anticipation and a real glow about the place. We all felt so connected to the hotel.

The dining tables were set with white damask tablecloths and centre lamps. Each table seated eight people, and there seemed to be hundreds of tables. The extra ducks, the casual waitresses, were waiting on the tables – there would be a big payout later, I thought. There was much talking and laughing, glasses clinking. It was all very intimate. Here was our dedicated audience waiting for us to be announced. They were sitting down in their seats now. The stage was set.

Suddenly the noise ceased and the banqueting lights went down. It was quiet, still. We were on. The footlights came up and the spotlights. It was dazzling. We were being introduced. Pam was in the wings giving last-minute instructions and encouragement. 'Good Luck girls,' she whispered. We went on stage smiling broadly and I could feel the warmth from the stage lights emanating up toward us; it was hot.

The familiar music played and we counted ourselves in. We all made the most of our fifteen minutes of fame. We danced as we had never danced before proudly and confidently in time to the music. We gave our best. Behind, the chorus line was doing their bit and as Gina, Liz, and I danced and turned, we saw them moving gracefully around the stage grinning from ear to ear like the Cheshire cat in Alice.

There they were, holding their silver moons high above their heads. Despite their drunken excesses they were still standing upright, thank goodness, another miracle. Their expressions and look of concentration as they danced was a rare treat. We had to repress our laughter until later.

The show was over all too soon. Everyone clapped loudly. 'More!' they called, or 'Encore!' and 'Hurrah!' We took our curtseys and bows, and then left the stage for the last time, feeling stage struck. We had stars in our eyes. It had all been gorgeous fun. Our public had liked us. Afterwards, the girls let their hair down as the revels got under way. This time we were drunk on success.

The staff manager took a cine film of the show and of our dance. He was a happy man and evidently delighted with the proceedings.

'What do you think of the show so far?' he asked our public; the gentlemen in their Saville Row dinner suits and the ladies in their haute couture gowns with diamond necklaces. We mixed in with the crowds and enjoyed getting the attention all evening and took photographs of each other in our stage costumes with our new Kodak Instamatic cameras.

VI

The next morning Harry, the head night porter, knocked on the door of room 550 to wake us up for work with an early morning call.

'Anna, Anna… Lucinda… good morning girls, it is six o clock,' he said, quietly tapping. The bedroom door was ajar, left open all night it seemed, and Harry walked in to find a state of utter confusion and turmoil. The room looked as if a bomb had hit it. The bedroom light was switched on and water was gushing from the washbasin tap; it looked like the washer had gone. We had left an ironing board and iron out and a tray of dishes, which he almost fell over.

Unaware of all of this chaos, we had continued to remain in a dreamless state of sleep, shattered from our debut into the world of show business. Once we heard the clatter we opened our eyes to find Harry looking bewildered at the mayhem in the room. He seemed preoccupied and really not his usual self. Later we found out why.

Earlier in the week a sack of mail from the hotel, the Christmas post, all of it, had gone missing. It had been ready to go over to the post office on Mount Pleasant, but it had not arrived. The bag had gone, disappeared off the face of the earth: Lost in transit. No wonder Harry was such a worried man. It was a total mystery and became an ongoing hotel saga over the weeks. We all called it 'the vanishing act of the night mail.' Nobody, it seemed, could shed any light on the subject.

There was a hue and cry about it and the house dick was brought in to investigate and ask questions. It was a puzzle that he couldn't solve. It was a complete mystery. Then the transport police arrived. They were frequently on hand and regular visitors at the reception desk, usually social calls, but they were always a reassuring presence.

In due course the mail bags turned up and all was revealed. It transpired that there had been some racing at Kempton Park and the mail bag was eventually discovered lying around McAllister's betting shop in Mount Pleasant. A favourite haunt, one has to say, of the hall porters who liked a smoke and the excitement of a good bet. The mail bag had been dumped there on the floor, hidden away and forgotten, left in the bookies all over the Christmas period. Very unfortunate really, as prior to Christmas it is quiet with racing only at tracks like Huntingdon, Lingfield, or Kempton.

Not only had the hotel post been lost, but no one received any Christmas cards. It was the New Year when it all came to light.

'Hey ho, what a palaver,' said Miss Davies in reception with a big grin appearing on her face.

'Indeed it was,' said Harry, relieved and happy once more.

And we all saw the funny side. It was a mishap; no real harm had been done.

VII

The day after the Christmas party and show everyone was anxious for a quick get away. Lucinda and I had said cheerio to our house guests then had to stop and pause for a domestic interlude in order to put the bedroom right and tidy it, which we did as quickly as possible. No chambermaid could have sorted it. By teatime we had just managed to pack our weekend bags, and then we ran like fury to catch the train. Lucinda was coming home with me.

It started to rain. Lucinda and I walked in silence along the road together from the station. It was calm, there was not much traffic. I noticed the stars scattered in the night sky as the moon shone damply down onto the rooftops below. Everything seemed a bit of a blur. Even my white umbrella had been left behind on the train.

From the end of the road we could see my home. In the window, tiny fairy lights twinkled on a small Christmas tree. It was traditional. Lucinda linked arms with me as we walked up the garden path, and she started singing carols in her lovely clear voice, which resonated in the cool night air. And I started to sing too.

VIII

On New Year's Eve in the hotel there was a grand dinner dance. It was quite a lavish affair, and guests came to spend the night; dinner, bed and breakfast rates applied. The guests were eager and ready to enter into the spirit of things. The dinner dance was held in the lounge, which was arranged to accommodate an orchestra and floor space for dancing.

The Christmas tree on the steps of the lounge added to the ambience and festive atmosphere, but the piece de resistance, the finishing touch on such a splendid occasion, was of a Scottish flavour. Hogmanay came to the Adelphi, and the sound of bagpipes could be heard from the rooftops! Without a doubt a very inebriated man in full regalia: highland kilt, sporran, the lot, piped in the New Year.

As midnight approached one memorable year, the Scottish piper slumped to the floor with a dirty great thud in a drunken stupor, unable to move. He fell onto his bagpipes, which made a resounding, most horrendous din as he lay paralytic on the ground, a dead weight, out for the count, until an assistant manager was paged and came to the rescue. Help!

Those working on reception were allowed to finish work just before twelve o'clock midnight. They would join the assistant managers in the penthouse suite on the sixth floor of the hotel, which was at the front of the building and overlooked Lewis's and toward the town. We stood outside on the veranda in the cold and surveyed the sights. This was when the Adelphi felt like the Buckingham Palace of Liverpool.

The ships and tug boats could be heard, and the familiar fog horns on the River Mersey not that far away. Church bells clanged out over the small city, welcoming the New Year. It felt exhilarating. Once twelve o'clock was over and the immediate hugging and shaking of hands had subsided, we would go, by kind invitation, to Miss Murphy's suite of rooms on the fourth floor.

How beautiful and welcoming her apartment looked. It was palatial and resembled a stately home. Her table lamps provided subdued lighting that fell gently on our young but by now ever so tired faces. We were invited to take some light refreshments and sample the most amazing selection of German goodies: iced ginger biscuits, dark chocolate hearts filled with jam, marzipan and other spicy delicacies that are commonplace today but then were unusual and different, a rare treat. After this we felt revived and talked into the early hours.

The festive season seemed to bring the staff closer together. There was a real sense of friendship, and everyone seemed kinder and more caring. Even when I revisit it, as seen through the misty eyes of my youth I still think it was a civilised and agreeable way to start the New Year; a good beginning.

CHAPTER FOUR
No Angels

I

Sometimes I woke up in the middle of the night in my hotel room and would lie in bed unable to sleep for thinking about my mother. My heart would pound as I tried to sleep but could not. I thought of C.S. Lewis when he wrote, 'No one ever told me that grief felt so much like fear.' And it did.

Lucinda often wasn't there. She was sometimes working late, or away visiting family. Gina and Liz, who shared a room opposite, started leaving their bedroom door open in the evenings and suggested I leave my door open too. They thought I might feel better if could hear them around. Being aware of their presence and with the bedroom light shining in from across the corridor, I did begin to feel easier. They were right; it was comforting.

Gina and Liz were good pals and full of life. They shared a room even though they were both worked on reception together. Gina, who was probably in her late twenties, maybe more, was feisty and had a habit of shaking her hair back in a provocative and affected manner. Liz was slightly younger, pretty and curvaceous, with rich dark brown hair that curled softly around her face and then fell gently onto the nape of her neck. She had a look of the film actress Clara Bow as she had appeared in, 'The It Girl,' especially when she rolled her eyes; the green eye shadow she wore helped to accentuate them.

Both were night owls, and they kept very late hours either being entertained or out partying. They claimed night times as their own and they would return to the hotel in the early hours with the dawn chorus.

Gina and Liz were both glamorous femme fatales, or (in the immortal words of the head bookkeeper), they were red hot tomatoes sirens who played fast and loose, enjoying the chase. They embraced the sexual revolution of the sixties. The advent of the contraceptive pill was liberating for some, and it came at the right time for those who wanted to embark on affairs or maybe take the initiative when the opportunity arose.

They were quite daring to live outside contemporary mores, although it did not strike me at the time. For Gina and Liz, falling in love was a major occupation. They had a sense of the romantic and liked to daydream about men, and their soon-to-be lovers. Both girls did much daydreaming, and their ambition was to get married. They wanted to find husbands, or more to the point, rich husbands. I had noticed there was no shortage of men dancing attendance on them. They had lots of admirers and seemed to get into the habit of falling in love at the drop of a hat.

Their late night mood music would quietly float out of their bedroom door along the corridor, background noise as they smoked and talked. Sometimes I could hear their hilarity, chatter, the clatter of coffee cups, or the sound of bath water running as they went to and from the bathrooms in their brightly patterned housecoats and fluffy indoor shoes, carrying potions and lotions to make themselves even more beautiful, more desirable.

Occasionally the smell of cigarettes would drift into my room, and I would be vaguely aware of all the comings and goings. It was good to have their company and be amongst them.

II

It became official that my room door was left open at night. It was allowed, so it became a sort of drop in centre, an open house, and all sorts of people would pop their heads round the door for a chat, to say hello, and keep me company. These soirees became a regular thing, and everyone made an effort to call, although it was usually quite late and often I would be ready for bed.

There was always a friendly face or a cheery voice. Mr Debonair, a permanent resident, would call in after his late evening meal to see how I was feeling; after all, he was part of the hotel family and most likely the hall porters knew of his whereabouts which made it alright. He brought a rose, and his brandy, up from the restaurant, and he sat relaxing, lighting a cigar, in an armchair in our sitting room.

'I've come to see how you are, Anna.' He puffed at the cigar.

'Fine, not too bad, thank you, still unable to sleep, an insomniac you know,' I replied, and he would raise a smile. He spoke like he had a mother.

I would have propped myself up with pillows, sitting up in bed, while Lucinda would have brought her creamy milk up from the lounge pantry. Together we listened to the lively banter and conversations going on around us. My hair would be tied back, brushed and washed and ready for the morning, my uniform pressed and hanging up on the wardrobe door, my clean face ready for sleep that never came.

III

Gina and Liz continued leaving their door open. For my part I was glad of their friendship and pleased to have them around. It felt normal even though they were nocturnal creatures.

They were usually the very best of friends, until one day there was an almighty row, a cat fight and the fur started flying, all over a man. This man had a reputation that has not often been matched. He had all the qualities they were looking for and more: rich, famous, handsome, talented, and attractive; a rising star. His recent hit single had unlocked the door to fame for him in the climate change of music in the sixties.

Women went wild for him. They would swoon and go delirious. He was well known for his blatant sexuality, his tight trousers, and billowing shirts. What it was to be iconic.

Gina and Liz both happened to be on duty at reception that day when this celebrated singer checked into the hotel and made a beeline for them, or was it vice versa? I don't think much encouragement was needed. Liz gave him the big eye and fluttered her long, lustrous eyelashes.

This pop idol was a hunk: a dish, a heartbreaker, and how fabulously thrilling to meet him in the flesh. The atmosphere was electric. Giving her a smouldering look, he asked her out on a date, arranging to meet her that night at the main entrance of the hotel. Liz couldn't believe her luck. She blinked, blown away.

Shortly afterwards his manager came to the front desk and unwittingly made a date (for him) with Gina; a blind date. The manager obviously didn't want his protégée to feel lonely after the show finished; women's company and entertainment was the order of the day. Gina's rendezvous was at the timekeeper's door at the side of the hotel.

Gina was so excited and couldn't wait to tell Liz the news that she had a date fixed up at the timekeeper's entrance. An elated Liz was equally longing to share her big news that she had a date at the front of the hotel, under the clock, at the main entrance. What a commotion and uproar, when realisation dawned. They were taken aback. Both had a date with this drop-dead gorgeous guy on the same night, at the same time; quite a coincidence.

There was much yelling, screaming, and shouting; neither would give way. They were no angels. The stakes were just too high. It *was* a big deal. He was hot stuff. So they decided to do the only decent thing and both go out with him; a double date, ménage a trios.

IV

Gina and Liz set about the business of preparing their big night out. They wanted to look their best, to feel attractive, seductive, and sexy. Everyone on the fifth floor convent wanted to be in on it, and the gossip spread quickly around the hotel and became more and more exaggerated as the tale was recounted.

The girls spent long hours getting ready. They looked intensely excited with shining eyes as they dressed slowly with care. They got heavily made-up: two coats of mascara, matching nail polish and lipstick, then a light film of face powder to add the finishing touch. Liz with the familiar kiss curls teased onto her face looked arresting as did Gina, who had a sleek bob that emphasised her strong profile.

They both emerged looking like models; very a la mode in their slinky, strapless cocktail dresses and tottering heels; vamps! And off they went with gay abandon on their one-night stand, to enjoy themselves in a make-believe world, fools for love.

So, we were left with these unforgettable images of what promised to be a historic moment in time as Gina and Liz tripped the light fantastic with a sex symbol of the sixties.

Outside my room it felt eerily still; the calm after the storm. My bedroom door firmly closed now, I felt tired and curled up into bed. I welcomed the prospect of a good nights sleep and so was not around to see their return.

But I saw it for myself the next day. They were in their own private paradise. Their looks said it all.

Soon afterward, Gina and Liz achieved their ambition and wish fulfilment. Romance became a reality and not just a vision. They gave in their notice and left the hotel. Each married wealthy men. Gina had fallen for an American who was a resident in the hotel, and off they went to live in the States. Liz also married a man who was a resident in the hotel. He was older and in trade; filthy rich. It mattered little. He was totally beguiled by her. And so, there they were, in love again.

You see, there was nothing quite like a husband as a natural progression route out of the hotel.

V

A new receptionist came to occupy the room opposite. She was called Jeanette and came from up north. She was different: more refined, a blue stocking and more highbrow an academic, but another night owl. Her private passions were classical music and jazz. She left her door open too, so we became good friends as well as neighbours. A few years later down the line, Jeanette fell hopelessly and helplessly in love. She left the hotel to get married, what else!

The marriage took place at St Nicholas' Church, the parish church of Liverpool. Keith was an assistant manager in the hotel. We referred to him as Frank Sinatra. He really looked like Frank.

CHAPTER FIVE
Boss Freely

I

Pat, as we called her, had worked all her life in British Transport Hotels. She came from Sligo in Ireland. Her mother and youngest sister still lived there in the family home, to which Pat sent a chunk of her wages every pay day. She had four Irish sisters. They all had their birthdays registered on the same day, June 10th, a job lot, as was sometimes the case when people lived in remote parts of Ireland.

Pat had the Irish colouring: lovely blue eyes the colour of cornflowers and thick, richly coloured dark brown hair. She wore this in a short, sort of bouncy style with curls. She liked it tidy, and once it was done she didn't bother with it. I noticed she had good, strong, teeth; like a horse I used to think.

She wore glasses that were more off her face than on. She would have them in her hands, perched on top of her head, or they would be left casually lying about, an accident waiting to happen. She had another habit of running her hands through her hair. This was while she was thinking before she spoke. She retained her strong Irish accent even though it was a long while since she had left the Emerald Isle.

II

Pat was a very modern and forward thinking boss. Unlike Miss Wilson, Pat's authority was based on goodwill. She always encouraged us to take more responsibility, and she wanted us to understand the whole spectrum of hotel life and learn all aspects of our job and hers.

'Dwarling,' she would say, mimicking others in a put on and exaggerated far back voice, 'Lets do this banking together and you will see how it is done. Is that alright dear?' So, we learnt more and more and got a better understanding of things, although the times they were a changing. National Cash Register machines were installed, and we had training on how to use them. Sticking stamps onto the back of cheques became obsolete. Then a chute was put in the office which sent telephone chits and dockets to us in a capsule, a tube thing. The biggest change of all came later on when the country went decimal. We all went to the Midland Hotel, Manchester, to train and learn about the new currency.

I noticed in the office Pat always used the initials B.F. in her receipt book.

'Excuse me Pat,' I asked one day, peering over her shoulder and looking at her initials, B.F. 'What is your name? Why are you not using P as your initial?'

'My name, dear? Bridget Mary Elizabeth Theresa Dymphna Anatracta Freely,' was her quick response. Everything she did was like that, immediate.

'Well Pat,' I replied, somewhat puzzled, 'so the B.F. stands for'— and before I could say another word she replied, 'Bloody Fool,' and we all laughed.

'By the way, Pat,' I said. 'While we are talking about names, my name has got an "e" on the end.'

'Okay,' she said, and when I looked she had written the 'e' at the end of my surname and left my first name as Ann. But as I got called so many different names in the hotel anyway – Anne, Annie and Anna – I just accepted it.

Pat was slightly touched, and her subsequent behaviour only confirmed what I thought, when one day I arrived on duty just as she was entertaining ten or more small, foreign looking men who had no understanding of English. They were standing in a group at the front desk, some with arms folded. The men were grinning and showing their teeth, nodding knowingly at each other, mesmerised by Pat's antics.

There she was, looking faintly comic, running from one end of the office to the other, hurling herself about, hands cupped underneath her chin, pulling faces, trying to enact a bout of wrestling. She was trying to convey how we in Liverpool had a stadium. Wrestling was a very popular sport and the stadium attracted the likes of Giant Haystacks and Jackie Pallow. I'll never know how Pat managed to keep upright and not trip up on the old linoleum in the office, but the continental wrestlers seemed duly impressed and enjoyed the ringside performance.

III

The Adelphi had a house dick, or detective, Alan Cashen. He was a fairly big, middle-aged guy straight out of a Raymond Chandler book: same uniform, double-breasted suit and trilby hat, which he would park casually on the desk in the office.

He came to take cheques and money to the bank. He was never in any particular hurry and would sit down and talk for hours to Pat while she got all the stuff ready. He would watch and wait, furtively glancing round at the hotel comings and goings. He would read the VIP lists and the weekly special business list and see if anyone of notability was staying. It was, after all, his concern to know who was resident and what was going on in the hotel.

It was because of the hotel dick that Pat first thought about having driving lessons. He put the idea into her head because his wife was having lessons with a local driving school. Pat took a keen interest and asked a great many questions and decided it was a good idea. Yes, maybe she would learn to drive, like the detective's wife.

At first she would come back animated and full of enthusiasm and talk about the lesson and how the driving instructor would take her to Sefton Park to practise. Nobody in the front office was especially interested. This was because we all lived in the hotel. None of the hotel staff came to work by car, except the stores manager, who had a Jensen Interceptor. Everyone else used their rail passes and enjoyed free rail travel.

The Adelphi garage was at the side of the hotel on Brownlow Hill, and the car jockey would drive the limousines, belonging to hotel residents, from on the front and put the cars away in the garage. It was only then that anyone was remotely interested in motoring and more likely than not, it was the type of car and, more importantly who owned it!

One afternoon, two or maybe even three years later, we were all working in the front office as usual when driving came up in the conversation. It emerged much to our amazement and disbelief that Pat was still taking driving lessons. Not only that, but she had never driven out of Sefton Park. Yes, she was still going round the lake. We gaped. What? Pat was still driving around Sefton Park Lake? She had never been out on the main road. Surely not!

'Sorry?' said Jeanette. Pat repeated what she'd said and yes, we had heard properly the first time. Pat seemed to think it was normal; normal for her maybe.

Miss Davies in her head receptionist role perhaps could say something to Pat, but what? It was deemed best to say nothing. So, driving became a taboo subject, and it was never mentioned after that. If it did come up again, the conversation was quickly turned round to something topical and safe, like British Rail.

IV

Pat had come from the Exchange Hotel, which was in the business area of Liverpool by Exchange Station. It was another British Transport hotel, though smaller and more homely. She loved her job there and the people. It was like a family, but she was brought to the Adelphi to take over as the head bookkeeper because the Exchange Hotel was closing. She was the right age and had vast experience in the company plus a wide knowledge of hotels. The staff had to be relocated somewhere. It was obvious she was the right person, although it was not her choice. She was cajoled.

Pat had spent her working life with British Transport Hotels up and down the country, from Gleneagles in Scotland, to the Midland Hotel in Manchester. At Gleneagles she would tell us there was nothing much to do unless you played golf, although apparently she had heard there were five abortionists in Auchterander who were kept busy. Pat, as a devout Roman Catholic, was shocked, and although she was not judgemental she did not approve. She knew everybody in the company, was well liked, and had a large circle of friends, but she had remained single as we all were. It was company policy.

We had heard that some of the girls working on the front desk in the Adelphi had had babies. It was never really talked about. We never delved into people's private lives. All of these babies were given up for adoption. Change had come in the form of the contraceptive pill, which was available on prescription for married women in the early 1960s, but it was not offered to single women until 1967; too late for them, with their unrequited love affairs, fated romances, and unwanted pregnancies.

'Farewell the tranquil mind; farewell content!' said Othello.

V

The second head bookkeeper at that time was very good at her job. She knew it inside out. She was as cool as a cucumber and never got flustered. She had worked in the Adelphi for a long time, and it was difficult for her to get used to a new boss with new ways of doing things and different ideas.

Miss Wilson had been her trainer, and maybe she thought the job as head bookkeeper should be hers after Willy left. But then the second was an unknown quantity, and one didn't automatically warm to her. When they were on duty together Pat would stare and watch the second who was in a trance-like state, closing one of her eyes while she was thinking, prevaricating…. allowing her luxurious, long wavy hair to fall over one eye like Veronica Lake. Pat always used to say she had a Veronica Lake hair-do. Pat was mesmerised by her and thought her strange. But the second didn't really care for her much and thought Pat talked through her hat most of the time anyway.

VI

Hotel life carried on uneventfully. The second was in charge of the duty rosters. Both the heads worked straight days, but the bookkeepers' duties varied and there were lots of different shifts and split duties. We liked the hours and the social mix.

The weekend began at Friday lunchtime, returning for duty on Monday at three thirty; or it started Saturday lunchtime, returning Tuesday. Half days were taken midweek when you had worked the weekend. On Fridays there was a ten thirty until seven o clock shift to cover the off duty.

And someone had to pay the wages out. Friday was pay day for the staff who clocked on into work.

A designated bookkeeper would go down to the kitchen office to pay the wages out with an assistant manager who marched on ahead carrying the brown wage packets and cash book in a wooden fruit and vegetable box. This paying out was between ten thirty, after the balance, until twelve o'clock every Friday. The staff would queue to collect their hard earned wages, sometimes making a special journey into town if it was their day off.

The bookkeeper paying out had to ensure staff signed for their wages next to their name in the cash book and check it against the name on the wage packet. This was harder than it sounds, as some of the staff had disabilities and difficulties and couldn't read or write. Then they would carefully put a cross next to their name instead of their signature, which was fine. The hotel was inclusive and exclusive at the same time.

Paying out the wages was a good chance to meet all the staff who were friendly, uncomplaining, and kindly. Everyone looked forward to pay day. It was an enormous staff, and occasionally things would go wrong and mistakes happened. Maybe there was no overtime included or holiday pay missed out, or perhaps the wrong pay packet had been given to someone with a similar name. The pig swill man also had to be paid. Often cutlery was lost, thrown in the swill by mistake, and the pig farmer would return it on his next trip.

The extra ducks, the waitresses, were an army of women: sisters, aunts, cousins, daughters, mostly Liverpudlians born and bred. They waited on at all the special business functions, and in many ways they were the stalwarts of the Adelphi. These extras, all casuals, were very smart and wore black dresses with white aprons. Their hair was always freshly set, off their faces. They were usually paid on a Friday night on production of their clock card after functions had finished. The bookkeeper on duty would pay out with the assistant manager and the head banqueting waiter/manager, Klaus or Brian. It was a team effort. This would be done on the mezzanine floor. For a smaller function with fewer staff, payment would be made in the front office.

The toastmaster easily stood out, dressed in a bright red jacket and wearing white cotton gloves. He would carry his toastmaster's gavel and come to the front desk for his fee, which was £10.0s.0d. paid out on a disbursement.

Sometimes there were *Upstairs Downstairs* moments when the extra waitresses would take umbrage in certain situations, like the time Cilla Black got married and the wedding reception was held in the hotel. Cilla was only very young and just starting off as a singer in her showbiz career. The ducks, snobs in their own way, grumbled at waiting on someone *not from Scotland Road!* But her husband-to-be,

Bobby Willis, was liked by absolutely everyone, and anyone who had a heart loved him too.

We all worked long hours for a small wage, and money was limited; it nearly always was, alas, alack! Pat insisted on us putting some money straight into the bank.

'You need, running away money,' she would say, so catching the bus up Brownlow Hill, two stops to Martins Bank, University Branch I dutifully deposited a tiny bit there for a rainy day: a new winter coat, a pair of shoes, or a holiday perhaps. Pat, on the other hand, did not practise what she preached, and would run across the road, putting only a small sum of her wages in the Allied Irish Bank for her mother, before going into Blackler's the department store and buying up the shop with the rest of it.

If the business was there, we all had to work and leave was cancelled. We were kept on our toes most of the time, as the front office was always busy and it was easy to make mistakes when such large amounts of money were involved. Sometimes you could be serving two, three, or even four guests at the same time, thinking they would be straightforward transactions when they often were not.

Errors occurred by misreading the exchange rates or looking at the rate for American dollars when they should have been Canadian. Often disbursements were mislaid and went missing, and floats vanished into thin air by doing too many things at once, simply by being too tired. We were often muzzy and thick headed with sleep, or rather, from lack of it.

Control, upstairs on the mezzanine, checked our work everyday. They checked till rolls against bills, and audit came to check the money. When this happened, if someone was short, we closed ranks and formed a line. Sindy who was now the second head bookkeeper would head the operation. In her laissez faire and flippant manner, she would stand by her drawer with attitude at the top of the line. The rest of the bookkeepers would take her lead and stand in tactical positions by their open desk drawers.

The receptionists did their bit to help by passing money haphazardly along the ranks in chain-gang fashion. The money was given to them by dear Rose Lewis, who ran theatre bookings and held the ticket money. She was black staff, her office being at the end of reception.

So Rosie saved the day by using her money to make good our floats, after which she would have to go for a smoke to steady her nerves. Once audit had left the premises we would give her the money back and Pat would make up any shortfall by going to the bank with the dollars and foreign currency and getting a good exchange rate. Pat made a friend of the bank manager at the Midland Bank at the bottom of Bold Street, and he would help us out when he could and kept us solvent.

If the shortfall couldn't be fixed, we sometimes resorted to using winnings from the Grand National or any tips we had in the kitty, although this never amounted to much, usually coppers. There was never any serious discrepancy, but had there been management would of course have been informed. The only time I can ever recall a major issue was when the country went on strike, during the social revolutions of the sixties, when the Labour Party was in office.

Like everywhere else in the country, the hotel would be without electricity; there was no lighting or heating, so there were times when we worked by candlelight in the cold and pitch black. It was especially bad on those dark winter mornings when it felt like the middle of the night and we couldn't see anything, let alone the colours of the bank notes or travellers cheques.

It was a hard and difficult time for many people and frustrating for us as it affected our working lives. We would resort to swearing in despair; but the boss, as we sometimes called her, would have no blaspheming or mouthing off. Woe betide anyone who did; out would come the swear box. 'It doesn't become you,' she would say and wrinkle her nose, 'especially you, little Annie,' though that did not stop her from saying 'bloody hell' and 'good God' when an expletive was needed.

She was deeply religious, a devout Roman Catholic, a daily communicant, and a great believer in St Anthony, patron saint of lost possessions. She frequently prayed to him. She would tell us of his merits, but she called him a 'due boy' because according to Pat, if you didn't pay your dues he would not intercede and help a second time. I can still hear Pat's voice with its native accent now, 'Do not forget the poor box, remember St Anthony's Bread.'

VII

Pat was familiar and friendly with many of the celebrities who came to stay in the hotel and would enjoy socialising with them and partying along with the rest of us. She was a huge fan of David Lean and liked his films. A particular favourite, though, was Ken Loach, who was doing a lot of political filming in Liverpool at that time. *The Big Flame*, which was about the Liverpool dock strike, and *Rank and File,* which dealt with issues around the Pilkington strike in St Helens. Earlier in the 1960s Ken Loach made homelessness a political issue, with *Cathy Come Home,* which inspired the charity shelter. Then in 1969 there was *Kes* by Barry Hines.

At times like these there would often be a soiree in one of the hotel suites or stockrooms, and sometimes we would have a running buffet and a bar. Pat would be on good form. She was very adept at bright, lively conversation, and she engaged easily with others, especially after a few snifters. She was not averse to a gin and tonic.

She adored the French assistant managers and trainees and would speak to them in broken French or in pigeon English with a French accent, which made us laugh. She was funny. She liked combining pleasure with intellectual conversation and she would introduce you to absolutely everyone.

Sometimes if there was too much pleasure going on, her 'mother hat' would magically appear with her *Railway Book of Rules* and you would have to do exactly as you were told and behave; that is, not slink off anywhere with anyone. Pat worried that our heads would become full of men, and if she didn't like a man or she thought he was odd she would refer to him as 'a gink'. And so, many an ideal opportunity of being picked up was missed.

VIII

Pat loved her food and she ate in the courier's room usually with the head telephonist. They would enjoy a good chinwag together. Jack Allen, the chef, looked after Pat, who would go into raptures over the delicious dishes he put before her. How she relished the beautifully cooked full English breakfasts, a la carte lunches, high teas in the afternoon with cream cakes and buttered scones, and tasty hot dishes for supper.

At first gaining a bit of weight did not matter, but we all noticed a difference in how we looked when our black dresses had to be discarded for the new uniforms. We would never again feel svelte and sylphlike as we had done in our blacks.

The new regulation uniforms were made-to-measure suits, and we all went for a fitting at the tailors. The suits matched the new British Rail colours and were a bluish green with a knee-length straight skirt and a box jacket in a thick woollen worsted material. None of us felt slim in this bulky new fabric.

As soon as we were able the hems on the skirts were shortened as high as we could get them, right up to the thighs, although we weren't supposed to personalise them. We had two suits and three white cotton blouses, which seemed to be drip drying forever after in the ironing room, and we all felt shapeless in them. They did not flatter us or show off our figures.

To try and combat any weight gain and improve our figures, a crowd of us, including Pat, Christine, Maureen, and I, joined May Cotterill's keep fit class in adult education. I stood watching, reading Pat's thoughts. Age was creeping up on her. She would slap her sides and look down at her solid and spreading waistline.

She did not like this feeling heavy, of being several sizes bigger, and so she started to eat smaller portions; too late… too late… a new age had dawned. Middle age had arrived.

CHAPTER SIX
Jules Misbehaves

I

The hotel was always full of engaging, affable characters with attractive personalities, mostly male. One resident who fitted this description who also had an amorous sounding name was an Italian called Mr Enrico Debonair. Some of the girls on the front desk knew him as Rico. He was a distinguished looking middle-aged man of Verona, Italy. One might say he was a typical Italian; handsome, swarthy, dramatically black haired, though it was thinning on the top, a high forehead, a Roman nose, and dark eyes. A regular Don Juan, he was skilled in charming others.

Mr Debonair resided indefinitely in room 301. He would check his bill thoroughly every week with the bookkeepers and query each item separately. He seemed to like the thrill of encountering new women staff on the front desk with their freshness and bright conversation, coupled with a naiveté that was appealing; he could also be deliberately exacting and difficult with them. First he would be facetious, and then he became every bit the volatile Italian with a real Latin temperament.

How much was he charged for this and that and did his Campari really cost—what—how much?

Next he would look at his telephone calls. We would have to search through the hundreds of phone chits until the originals were found and then make any necessary adjustments to his bill. And so it would go on. In fairness, sometimes items were incorrectly posted on room 301. Mistakes were made. His response would be in Italian, which none of us could understand, but you could easily get the drift.

During the day Mr Debonair was working on a prestigious building project in Liverpool. He was the engineer. One of his previous commissions was an innovative new building in London, that's how illustrious he was and so he was much sought after. Today it would be referred to as head hunted.

He would leave the hotel very early each morning for work, so it was in the evening, usually after he had dined in the French restaurant, that he would come to the front desk and say good evening. Mr Debonair would come seeking female company and to chat. He would look suave, dashing even, wearing beautiful Pierre Balmain shirts, jackets, aftershave, and Italian hand-made leather shoes. He had impeccable dress sense and flawless manners. He would never come into the foyer empty handed but would bring a fresh rose taken from the restaurant and present it to one of the receptionists or bookkeepers who would be at the desk working on the late shift.

'Thees is for you, justa for you,' he would say in a seductive, caressing tone, and one would feel he had singled you out.

'Don't you think he's rather attractive, you know, in a sophisticated sort of way?' I overheard Patsy saying to Lucinda, and they laughed.

'Yes I suppose so,' Lucinda replied. And there we all were looking at him, smiling, bewitched by his magnetic charms.

II

The late shift always had an element of fun and spontaneity. It was usual for the girls going on duty at three thirty to get up a bit later in the morning, pull on some clothes, and meet *en famille* in the stewards' room, which is where we had our meals. It was nice to share meal times together and catch up with hotel news. It was very sociable.

The early part of the afternoon was largely spent getting ready for work. We had to pace ourselves, because even though we were young women it was a long haul working until midnight. Getting ready for work entailed a trip to the hairdressers, and there was always a craze: hair pieces, false eyelashes, eye lash curlers, false nails, and so on. This was the swinging sixties, after all, and it was great to be young; even if young and foolish.

In the evenings the duty managers and a large number of male staff wore black tie, as was the dress code. This was the norm when there were so many special business events taking place. These very high profile functions were held in the many public rooms in the hotel, which had been designed to compare with the first class areas of the Cunard liners and to accommodate the transatlantic business.

They symbolised greatness. Just to stand back and gaze upward at the decorative ceilings lit by chandeliers, the huge nests of bright lights, was an experience in itself. These lovely rooms would be filled with a glow, and an air of expectancy; they reflected the trappings of an enviable lifestyle left over from another era.

Our hotel manager immaculately dressed in his dinner suit wore a fresh red rose in his lapel. He was always a punctual, totally unflappable, and a familiar figure in the front hall. You could usually find him beaming, ready to receive and welcome guests graciously across the threshold. He came from a class that was the very essence of Englishness.

We followed his lead. It was so very much part of the job to look one's best and have a sense of occasion. We had to dress appropriately too, in those days, still wearing our best black dresses, which were simple and sensual made in the finest jersey wool, or crepe. Everyone wore different styles and accessories to offset the black.

It was on such an evening shift with romance in the air that Lucinda formed an attachment with Mr Debonair, the Italian gentleman, and the friendship blossomed.

Lucinda would be sitting on one of the high stools at the front of reception, and Mr Debonair would come down the staircase from the lounge and give her a long, lingering look, and she would dissolve and go round in a trance of happiness.

III

So, it did not come as any great surprise when he asked Lucinda out, to accompany him to the theatre no less, to see the opera *La Traviata*; a heavy date. Getting ready was half the fun. The agony of anticipation and what to wear! Well, she bought the most beautiful pale pink satin dress from an expensive boutique in Bold Street. It was beautiful, a perfect fit, and just right for the opera. It had a high neck with a slight frill, edged with velvet. The detail was quite something. It hung wonderfully well in a sort of flair and rested above the knee. Her naturally blonde hair was done up with wispy curly bits pulled and teased around her ears. The effect was pale and interesting.

Lucinda had a perfectly wonderful time. The evening was everything she had imagined it would be and more. She played the music from Verdi's opera in our room over the next few days. If love songs provide a language of love then *La Traviata* did it for her. It was such a popular and passionate love story of the nineteenth century, and we became au fait with the arias and songs in the opera. We all waited with bated breath for Mr Debonair to ask Lucinda out again.

He did, of course, ask her out, and the dates, the outings, and romance continued for a time. However, all good things must come to an end, and Lucinda had other ideas.

I had known from the start that she would not stay long at the Adelphi, and when a vacancy came up she transferred to another British Transport Hotel, the Great Northern Hotel London. Lucinda loved London! Later she found a position abroad as an au pair girl in Berlin, which had been part of her original long-term plan. And so she embarked on a lifetime of travel and adventures which took her to exotic places and distant continents.

IV

Meanwhile, Mr Debonair was still very much a resident and part of the everyday scene at the Adelphi. He kept to his routine of dining in the French restaurant late in the evening and then coming to the front desk, where he would engage in pleasant conversation. He befriended Julia, who had come to replace Lucinda. Julia conversed easily with him. She was a bit older and more a woman of the world. Jules liked to enjoy herself. She liked a drink, smoked cigarettes, and was not shy. She would go to room 301 to keep him company and because she liked him.

I went with her, just once, after we finished work. It was out of curiosity. I had hesitated but could not resist the invitation to look at room 301. The Adelphi rooms were all slightly different, and it was interesting to see how the interiors varied. I thought it was very daring and bold, and undoubtedly foolish of course. It was not permitted to visit residents' bedrooms like this, but caution was thrown to the wind as we sneaked up to the third floor after midnight. Room 301 was tastefully and exquisitely designed. It felt almost continental, spacious, with no clutter. The furniture was so beautifully and carefully placed.

The floor was so smoothly polished it looked like glass, and you could see your reflection in it, so we felt obliged to leave our shoes by the door.

I glanced around for somewhere to sit. Julia had already parked herself on the bed, and Mr Debonair was getting her a drink. Noticing his record collection I asked if I might borrow the LP *Dr Zhivago*.

'Yes, Anna, of course,' he said, inclining his head towards the bed for me to sit down, and he took his pen and wrote on the sleeve, 'my name is Jack…. I want it back.' Then he came over and joined us.

Julia said she was tired and cold and slid underneath the eiderdown, quite at home with her drink and cigarette in either hand. I wondered if she had been there before. But then it was her way to make herself at home; she was a friendly type. I stared randomly at the shoes.

I began, 'Come on Julia!' Then again, 'Julia, don't fall asleep, we are on early in the morning, a quick turn around. Quickly finish your drink. It's late!'

She said nothing, but finished her whisky and cigarette in a daze, then did as I asked, though slowly, because she was tired and sleepy.

'Don't forget your shoes,' I said, not wanting to hang around. Would she never sit up and move herself off the bed?

Once outside 301, we lowered our voices and spoke conspiratorially together and made a run for it. We sped along the corridors as softly as we could on the deep pile carpets and then went stealthily up the main staircase, glancing furtively about. I noticed Jules was carrying her high heels in her hand as we stole along, not wanting to be seen or heard; like thieves in the night.

V

The next day Mr Debonair came to the reception desk at eight o'clock in the morning before he left for work and sought me out.

'Anna, Anna my little friend, I am so sorry you had to rush off last night.'

'Sorry, whatever for? We didn't intend to stay so late. Thank you for lending me the LP *Dr Zhivago*.' I passed it off nonchalantly, shrugging my shoulders and smiling.

'Keep it Anna, enjoy it. I want you to have it.'

He continued to be friendly with us all on reception. He never seemed to lack admirers. One day when he came to check his bill at the cashier's desk he said he was going home on holiday soon to Verona, in the north of Italy, and how much I would like it. It all sounded very cultured, very innocent, the city of Romeo and Juliet, the most famous lovers in history, picturesque squares, fashionable shops and Renaissance buildings.

On the morning of his departure he came back to the desk and asked 'Anna, Anna, come with me? We could meet Lucind-dah,' he leaned over and whispered persuasively. I hesitated. It would be wonderful to see Lucinda again. I was missing her so much.

I was about to answer him, vaguely aware of the receptionists and bookkeepers listening in on the conversation. They seemed to be gravitating now toward the window in the front office, and I wondered what the hullabaloo was all about. They were staring at a car, Mr Debonair's brand new car.

It was a Lamborghini, a green Lamborghini Espada. I turned and looked, thinking, *how nice.* We had heard it was a limited edition, one of only 186 models, and there it was, standing on the hotel forecourt:

Before I could answer him the matter was taken immediately out of my hands by Pat, who was sitting at her desk. I thought she was working, but she was no fool and nothing escaped her: she didn't miss a trick.

She didn't want her girls going down the slippery slope. The hotel banking paled into insignificance. She felt responsible. She liked Lucinda and me. We would be innocents abroad. Now, not being big on tact, she challenged him. Tapping the end of her pencil very loudly on the desk she said, 'I beg your pardon'.

Pat, remember, could represent mother, aunt, sister, or friend; with me it was usually mother. More like Mother Superior. Anyway, with her mother hat firmly in place once more, she moved like sheet lightning, shot out of her chair, leaving thousands of pounds strewn about the desk, and walked deliberately over to the counter to where Mr Debonair was standing. She was not taken in by this handsome Italian whose glint in the eye she recognised as lust. She knew that men were capable of loving more than one woman at once; the glasses were off now, and so were the gloves. No nonsense here.

'No,' she said firmly, 'little Annie is not going anywhere.' Then full of mother love she turned to me and rather sternly instructed, 'Get on with your work now *dear*!'

She was met with scorn, of course, from him. Debonair was silent, suppressing his annoyance, though you could have cut the atmosphere with a knife. How he loathed and detested this Irish woman, her interference and meddling. She lacked finesse.

He sneered and looked down his nose at her, fuming and inwardly seething; his chiselled features twisted. Then he turned on his heels, stuck his Roman nose in the air, and walked out of the revolving doors onto the Adelphi forecourt. Everybody stood motionless now and watched him go. We peered through the window as he got into the car, the green Lamborghini, and watched him drive away.

For a while at least things settled down and got back to normal. Then a post card arrived from Lucinda in Berlin. She was enjoying her job, learning German, making new friends, and having a good time. Then funnily enough another postcard arrived from Mr Debonair in Paris. It was a beautiful black and white photograph of Pont Neuf taken by Albert Monier.

And so that was *arrivederci* to the gentleman of Verona, for a while anyway.

CHAPTER SEVEN
Paris Is Divine

I

Everyone who was employed by British Transport Hotels had rail travel concessions. Staff took advantage of these fringe benefits and travelled as much as possible while they had a job in the company. We were quite an adventurous lot. The sixties was a time when more and people were starting to take holidays abroad.

To get your free tickets you gave your holiday dates to Mrs Fitz in the staff office. She would then check your leave entitlement and fix up the train tickets. It couldn't have been easier. Rail tickets were used to visit friends and family who were scattered about the English towns and countryside. One soon became au fait with rail travel. And going abroad was something else. It was novel, and using the free tickets was amazing.

I decided to explore Paris with my friend, Chris, who was already a seasoned traveller. Travelling to Paris by train, exploring foreign parts, and taking on the guise of a tourist was a completely new experience though. We wanted to see the sights and soak up the atmosphere of the capital city. We met in London Euston Station and caught the night boat train, travelling from Victoria Station via Newhaven and Dieppe.

We arrived at Gare St Lazare eager, excited, and full of anticipation. It was so different.

The main line railway station and surrounding streets on the way to our accommodation had unfamiliar noises and aromas: the strong smell of freshly made coffee, freshly baked loaves of bread, garlic, and the addictive smell of Gauloise, Camel, and Citane cigarettes pervaded the air. The Parisiennes at a glance looked very fashionable, and one caught a whiff of French perfume from passers-by on the street. It was a whole new culture. We were on the continent; on French soil.

Our rooms were near Gare St Lazare. Without wasting a moment we went out to explore Paris by night. What an adventure. I made my mind up without a moment's hesitation. Paris was divine.

II

The Champs-Elysées seen for the first time at night left a long and lasting impression: the neon lights, the fast traffic with a great many unusual cars and different types of vehicles, all hurtling along at breakneck speed. There was such a big clash of excitable foreign voices. It was all so strange and new. Our school girl French had not prepared us for this. It had no bearing on real life.

The variety of shops and cafes displaying mouth-watering selections of gateaux and pastries were very tempting. We enjoyed this night time window shopping. There was altogether too much to look at as we walked for miles and miles along the tree-lined avenues and moonlight-drenched boulevards. We soaked up these broad vistas until, completely exhausted, we made our way back.

Our Michelin guide to Paris told us everything we needed to know. As tourists we took in all the sights: the Folies Bergere, the Louvre, the River Seine, the Paris Metro, the Eiffel Tower and all the fashion houses. We revived our interest in French history. We read up and gleaned as much information as we could and absorbed it all like sponges.

We returned to London enthralled and in love with the French city. Then clutching our Paris *Match* magazine, a copy of Paris *Vogue*, and citron presse, we went our separate ways. I travelled back to Liverpool and the hotel.

III

The next time I went to Paris on a free train ticket was with Lucinda. She was still with the company, working in the Great Northern Hotel, London. So we met there and travelled through the night again, this time catching the boat train from Victoria, crossing from Dover to Calais and arriving at Gare du Nord.

The boat trains were overcrowded, and we were all packed tightly together like sardines. It didn't much matter. It was interesting watching people, talking to them, finding out about things.

Arriving in Paris, we stayed with the nuns at Notre Dame Convent. Another convent! But this one was a lot different. It had no mirrors, for one thing. Lucinda and I felt somewhat dishevelled and the worse for wear from our long overnight journey. So it was with tousled hair and well-scrubbed, shiny faces from a good dousing in the freezing cold water at the convent that we discovered Paris. And it was even more divine second time round.

First of all we climbed the 385 steps to the top of Notre Dame Cathedral and looked out over the city. We thought the views breathtaking and from the tiny platform spotted various landmarks.

Later in the Latin Quarter, we sampled delicious coffee in huge cups with freshly made croissants that we dipped into the steaming coffee like everyone else. Then we climbed another lot of steps at Montmatre and Sacre Coeur. Oh how we enjoyed the panoramic views and basking in the continental atmosphere. Artists stood casually around with their paintbrushes and easels, painting and sketching, while others sat strumming on their guitars outside on the pavement.

We had friends in Paris from the Adelphi. Val worked on the same shift as Lucinda and Olwen. She was someone else with an ambition to travel and use her knowledge of languages. The job as a receptionist at the Ambassador Hotel on Boulevard Hausemann provided her with this opportunity, and she became fluent in French. She was pleased to see us even if it was only a fleeting visit.

The other friends we met were young trainee managers with British Transport Hotels getting work experience in Paris. They worked at Le Fouquet's Restaurant, not far from the Arc d'Triomphe on the Champs Elysee and others worked at the Georges Cinq Hotel. There was a whole group of trainees, and they seemed very pleased to see our familiar faces from Liverpool. Of course they had seen some turbulent times in Paris with the riots, but we saw nothing of these. And for part of our stay they showed us around Paris quite proudly.

We took in the many museums, galleries, cafes, and a bar where a moustachioed barman pulled a pistol out because we said Napoleon was Italian. We saw a cockerel fight and dawn coming up while we ate brown onion soup at Les Halles. One evening Lucinda and I ate out in an authentic French restaurant which Mr Debonair had recommended. He made the reservation for us. It was a good way to end our visit to Paris.

Back on terra firma in England we had morning coffee in style at Fortnum and Mason before returning to work in our separate hotels.

IV

British Transport Hotel employees were entitled to two weeks holiday a year. But sometimes we accumulated time-owing from working bank holidays, or for doing overtime. This could be added on to days off, making a long weekend stretch into a week.

Using the privilege rail tickets one could travel about and see something of this country too. We had turned into clones of the American tourists who frequented the hotel with their guide books and itineraries. We took in Cornwall and the West Country, Scotland, Ireland, and Wales.

London became familiar and we became at home around the great metropolis. We liked the big department stores and marvelled at Kensington High Street shops, especially Biba, where we would spend hours and hours window shopping. It was just so good to be there in 'The Smoke'. It was mostly weekends when one managed to get away to London. A day trip was not unheard of either now that we had the high-speed Pullman trains. There need be no real reason to visit the capital city except perhaps to meet a friend for coffee, buy some

Christmas presents, catch a show, or visit a gallery. Sometimes there was a party.

Train journeys, travel, and timetables were part of life at the Adelphi. We were a railway hotel, after all. Our livelihood, to a degree, depended on the trains. It was interesting telling tales and swapping stories; talking and touching on things, sharing interests and experiences. It gave staff common ground and was usually done over a cup of tea or on a meal break in the stewards' room.

We were an authority on railway matters, and what an undeniable romanticism about train travel there was then. It was a fabulous time: a phase of endless energy, enthusiasm, and vitality; a desire for knowledge, adventure, fun, and forging friendships.

CHAPTER EIGHT
A Special Occasion

I

The Grand National at Aintree Racecourse was an occasion rather than just a race. It always followed the Cheltenham Festival in March and would fall either in the weeks before or just after Easter.

In the very beautiful and capable surroundings of the Adelphi Hotel the event burgeoned. The Grand National event filled the Adelphi, Liverpool's most popular choice; it was certainly the talk of the town, especially among the Irish racing fraternity who descended into Liverpool in the thousands. The other hotels, restaurants, and pubs in Liverpool would take the overflow and joined in the celebrations as well.

The Grand National race meeting was held over three days; it began on Thursday with the big race taking place on Saturday. It was exciting watching the guests as they arrived at the hotel. They travelled to Liverpool by car, train, boat, and aeroplane. The hotel foyer was crowded as the hoards checked in and registered at reception, collecting room keys and messages, with the porters a few steps behind carrying luggage. Familiar faces greeted each other like long lost friends and people, stood about talking nineteen to the dozen. The place was full of lively banter and noise; pandemonium and chaos reigned.

In the front hall a notice was pinned up giving the names of the local Roman Catholic churches and the times of mass each day. Other denominations were listed as well. Guests noted this as they stood about waiting for the lifts to go to their rooms or suites of rooms. Everywhere was a jumble of people: jockeys, owners, trainers, valets, sports people, royalty, the racing press, and celebrities.

The Adelphi was the domain of the upper classes, high society and those who were well connected. It was the tribal home of gentlemen, and the excited race goers filled the hotel. Everyone dressed smartly and stylishly for all types of weather, because the weather could so easily vary. Sometimes at the National there would be blue skies and sunshine, at other times it snowed. It was often cold, windy, and wet, but it mattered little to the enjoyment of the event.

II

Preparation for the Grand National began as soon as the previous one was over; as guests checked out they would book for the following year. In the months leading up to the race meeting each head of department had arrangements to make and much planning and preparation. This was always done well in advance. All the departments in the hotel had to recruit staff in order to cope with, and meet the requirements of, the strenuous workload; and take stock to make sure there was enough of everything to meet the scale and demand of the occasion.

Menus would have been discussed in the kitchens with chef, and tradesmen would be delivering mountains of fresh produce: fruits and vegetables, salads, rounds of beef, saddles of lamb, fillets of veal, hams, chickens, and lobsters. The pastry chef and bakers would be working non-stop anticipating the day's business and making delicious confectionary: delicate mille feuilles and puff pastries, sumptuous meringues using great quantities of cream, exquisite chocolate éclairs. Mouth-watering stuff, these desserts were something else.

The hotel would empty after lunch each day, which enabled staff to prepare for the evening rush when everyone returned from the racecourse. In addition to the hotel guests, Liverpool people would fill the bars and restaurants over the three days and join in the extravaganza, particularly in the evenings.

III

During the Grand National, hotel routine went to pot. A typical day in the American bar would begin very early in the morning before opening for business at nine o'clock with Buck's Fizz. This was usually Moet and Chandon champagne with the juice from freshly squeezed oranges and was by far the most popular drink. Sometimes a Bloody Mary would be an alternative selection. This drink was made with vodka, tomato juice, and a dash of Tabasco sauce and Worcester sauce, with just a touch of fresh lemon juice, served with a stick of celery.

The bar would be hectic, and everyone would have a newspaper to read, the *Sporting Life*, the *Irish Times*, and the usual daily papers. About twelve o'clock the bar would empty and the guests would leave for the racecourse fortified. But then the staff would start again and be busy replenishing the shelves in readiness for the evening onslaught, a marathon session.

The wine cellars were under ground beneath the hotel, a massive area with corridors and walls, which were made of sandstone and very cool an ideal temperature in which to keep all the wines. The bottles of wine were stored in the mesh wine bins. The departments placed their orders with the head cellar man, who would then see that the wine was delivered promptly.

In the evenings, the bar would be heaving after the races, and guests would drink until three o'clock in the morning or even later. They would drink whisky, brandy, magnums of champagne, or Black Velvet, which was Guinness and champagne or champagne cocktails. These were made with a sugar lump placed in the bottom of the glass, then two or three drops of angostura bitters were added – which although made from herbs is alcoholic – followed by a measure of brandy and topped up with the champagne. As the sugar lump dissolved there was extra fizz, more sparkle to the champagne. The drink was quite popular as it had a little bit more kick to it. Some guests liked their drinks served at room temperature, and others liked chilled champagne. They would stir the drink with a champagne mosser, more commonly known as a swizzle stick.

Guests would congregate at the bar and pick at the nibbles, the dishes of peanuts, or the cheese biscuits. The topic of conversation naturally was racing, more specifically 'the race' and the excitement of the day's events: backing horses and winners, the prices, the going, and the form. It was a forum for telling many apocryphal tales and a time for drinking, enjoying, and being amongst the racing family dynasties. The bar was like a fog with thick smoke from all the Havana and Jamaican cigars. It smelt strongly of liquor and was packed to the gunnels throughout the event.

IV

In all the other parts of the hotel everyone would be mad busy with their own jobs, not least with replenishing the masses of bedroom, bathroom and table linens. In the kitchens it was non-stop too. There were hundreds upon hundreds of dishes: plates of all shapes and sizes, canteens of cutlery, and such a variety of glasses; ten- and twelve-ounce tumblers, flutes, four-and five-ounce balloons, schooners and an old-fashioned glass for American cocktails that would be used during the three-day meeting. More people were engaged to wash all the additional glasses and other 'extras' (ancillary staff) taken on for various duties.

The two hotel valets, Mr Jones and Mr Hickey, were instantly recognisable in their striped waistcoats, pocket book and pencil in hand as they came to the desk to bill accounts. They would have been kept busy throughout the event pressing trousers and shirts, making sure clothes were hung or laid out properly in rooms. Meanwhile, the electricians would be checking electrical equipment, lighting, and so on. The hotel cleaners would be working on every floor, taking advantage of this quiet period when the hotel had emptied to restore its polished sparkle.

The few front office staff left on duty in the afternoon when there was a lull in the event would rush upstairs to the residents' television room on the mezzanine and watch the Grand National. After the race had been won, feeling completely exhausted, a spent force and shadows of their former selves, the girls would stagger off duty to get some sustenance and then sleep for a few hours.

Oh the tiredness! It was unbelievable, but sometimes a change of scenery away from the hotel helped. Sometimes we would walk along the road to one of the cinemas, where it was wonderful to unwind, sitting there in the dark and escape into a fantasy film world. It had to be the first house, of course, in order to get back to the hotel and early to bed.

Staff would exist on very little sleep over those three days. Many of the hotel staff would not even bother going home and would stay, grabbing a few hours rest before recommencing duty. Everyone would muck in, doing other people's work and helping each other whenever possible. There was a real sense of community spirit.

V

The Grand National celebrations culminated in a massive ball on Saturday night. It was probably more interesting to work late. There was such a tremendous atmosphere with boisterous drinking parties, lots and lots of money being spent, and everyone out to have a good time.

A superb buffet would be laid out in the main banqueting suite, served by chefs who would be well-scrubbed and wearing pristine uniforms complete with toque. Every table would contain chocolate horses iced in the winning owner's colours. There would also be ice sculptures, choux pastry, and all sorts of amazing spectacles. The festivities would continue until the early hours on the Sunday morning. It was an epic.

Next morning in the front office the girls would just be going off late duty as the early morning shift began their duty at six thirty sharp. They would have worked through the night ceaselessly, and the office would be in disarray because of the sheer volume of work. The early shift had the business of posting the early morning teas and breakfasts onto the room bills before the main checkout. They needed fresh eyes and vision to sort out any mess or queries that had been left and needed to be dealt with.

Queries happened all the time as guests came to pay their accounts, which would be astronomical amounts of money. They liked to double-check the totals and have the bill itemised. Guests who had taken luncheon hampers, which were of astonishing proportions, may have forgotten exactly what they ate, but everything imaginable was packed into the hampers: delicacies such as game pies, cold meats, and fish dishes, desserts, and fine wines. Then there was the crockery, silver, white linen napkins, and champagne flutes, because champagne was a must.

The floor waiter who prepared the hampers was responsible for billing the room accordingly, and he would have to make sure it was sent to the bookkeepers in good time before the guests checked out of the hotel. Sometimes, to be on the safe side, the floor waiter would telephone the amount through to the bookkeeper, and the onus was now on them to post it directly onto the account.

There was lots of extra business, such as the chance breakfasts and dressing rooms for people coming over on the Irish boats to bathe and change. Reception would also be up to their eyes with room allocations and housekeeper queries, but everyone rose to this special occasion. It was fatal to get a cold or feel below par when it was the Grand National as there was no respite, no let up. It was 'all go.'

Sometimes things became tense when guests came to check out and realise the fantastic amounts they had spent; crunch time. But we never panicked. Boss Freely and the rest of us could hold our own with aristocracy and were not intimidated by titled people, their cut glass accents, or staggering wealth. We never felt out of our depth.

The boss was shrewd, and her blunt manner or directness was quick to sense human folly. Of course she enjoyed meeting her fellow countrymen and hearing the lovely Irish accents, laughter, and gaiety, and she would revert to type and slip easily into the vernacular.

'Good Lord,' she would say when she saw how much had been drunk and by whom, or 'Between you, me, and the gatepost, he didn't stay by himself in that room.'

I think she must have kissed the Blarney Stone by the way she talked incessantly. She certainly had the gift of the gab, and there were lots of hilarious moments.

We all had our favourite Grand Nationals. Olwen's favourite and the one that stood out for her was the 1968 National when Gregory Peck stayed and his horse, Different Class, which was the favourite, came third.

In the 1980s the Grand National race meeting had an upsurge and saw rejuvenation after the course and land were sold by George Davies. *The Sun* newspaper took up sponsorship of the race.

It was later sponsored by Hennessey Cognac. The Hennessy family, headed by the managing director, Patrick, would stay at the Adelphi Hotel during the three day race meeting. The Adelphi, steeped in history and tradition, lent itself to the occasion and basked in the glory.

CHAPTER NINE
Behind The Scenes On Reception

Dear Lucinda,

Guess what! The Royal Ballet is staying here all week with Margot Fonteyn and Rudolf Nureyev! It has been thrilling. I got Rudolph's autograph. I could not stop myself, Lucinda. I had to ask him. I heard my voice saying, 'Please may I have your autograph?' I probably said 'Sir', as I know I would not have said 'Rudolph'.

 The principal dancers, their teachers, and managers congregate in the foyer, so there has been lots of hustle and bustle and excitement. It has never been so busy. Margot has been phoning her husband in Panama from the phone boxes in the foyer. So we have seen a lot of her. Do you remember, Lucinda, he was shot?

 Yesterday Mr Berry allowed *me* to attend a symposium in the hotel. The ballet company hosted it, and Margot gave a lecture. It was simply wonderful. Just to be there amongst them. I nearly fainted with excitement, so many icons. I pretended I was a dancer too. Yes, I know, I am thin enough!

Margot and company eat in the French restaurant after performances and stay late sitting in the alcoves around the tables, in the lamp light, smoking and talking. Dick Steele was playing beautifully as usual. And it is oh so amazing there. I collected the bills several times from the restaurant during the evening just so I could catch a glimpse of them.

Well, another bit of good luck, Olwen was given complementary tickets for the ballet, *Swan Lake*, good seats, front circle, so we are really looking forward to the performance. No doubt Ollie will dress up to the hilt for the occasion, which will be fun.

Margot has a beautiful chignon at the nape of her neck.

Tons and bundles of luv,

Anna

Dear Lucinda,

Great excitement here! Patsy and Sindy heard from the housekeepers today that the pop stars and supporting cast, who are staying in the hotel this week (they are appearing in twice nightly shows at the Empire), have brought a large wardrobe, racks and racks of the most beautiful stage clothes.

The clothes are hanging up all around their suite of rooms. So many different gowns made of gorgeous fabrics: silks, satins, chiffons, and velvets in so many colours and the styles. The housekeepers said it was a fantastic collection and not to be missed.

So, you will never guess. Patsy and Sindy took the keys for the suite from reception, and I went with them so we could see for ourselves. It was unbelievable! The suite of rooms resembled a department store, a fashion house. There were so many pairs of shoes and accessories, then racks and racks of dresses.

We did not stay long as we shouldn't really have been there but the housekeepers knew and didn't mind. Feeling somewhat guilty we closed the door and running for the lift got back to the reception desk before we were missed.

Look out for the review of the show in the paper.

Write soon!

Tons and bundles of love

Anna

Dear Lucinda,

 How is life in Berlin? Are you able to understand more of the language these days? Do send me a postcard soon.

 Oh Lucinda, after zis yer u vil hav a reli sensible styl. Zer vil be no mor trubls or difikultis and evrun u vil find it ezi tu understand ech ozer and ze drems vil finali kum tru!

 What do you think of my German?

Auf Weidersehen

*Ann*a

Dear Lucinda,

Your favourite person checked in the Hotel today. Eartha Kitt.

Love Anna

P.S. We have been given tickets to see Julian Bream at the Phil and last week; Daniel Barenbohim was here. More concerts; what joy.

Dear Lucinda,

Today Kensington Palace rang my house! Oh no, not Kensington Palace! I do not jest. What a shock!
The telephone call came just as I was expecting the dentist to ring. It was Lord Snowdon's personal secretary inviting me to a photographic exhibition at Kensington Palace.

I am not certain if the invitation meant meeting HRH as well. But do you remember my telling you how Tony, sorry, Lord Snowdon, had done some fantastic work for the *Times* on location in Africa and in *Vogue* magazine? And an article and photos of George Melly; can you recall it?

Lord Snowdon stayed at the Adelphi quite recently, still working for the *Times*. Well, I told him how much I was interested in photography, 35-mm, stills, etc., positives and negatives, and so on. I talked to him about my photographs and photo grams in sepia. He was really kind, and he listened. It was very interesting. I had to tell him my camera is only an old Fed! I was mortified.

Love Anna

P.S. Will you come with me to London, to the Palace? RSVP

Dear Lucinda,

The hotel has been busy. We have had lots of tours in from America. Your sister rang. She is going to live in New York. She saw a job in *The Lady* magazine.

Bye for now, Anna

Lucinda:

'Good evening sir, please can you register? Thank you. Hello, you're an American? Can you complete the alien form? This pink form; it's for aliens. Here it is. Now, what name did name did you say? I didn't quite catch it. Can you copy that, sorry, repeat it? Bill Anders? What! So, you've just flown in… from the moon? You've been orbiting in outer space! Oh yes, and please can I have your autograph for my friend Anne on bookkeepers? Sorry, I didn't catch what you said, sir. Got it.'

'Excuse me, Maureen, 'The astronaut, Bill Anders, is here. May I have some silver coins for him to take back home to America as a memento, please?'

Maureen

'Yes, of course, that's fine, but has he any moon dust we can have?'

Patsy:

'Good afternoon Miss —. Thank you for your booking and

176

confirmation for the room, Miss —. We understand from your manager that you require a second bedroom, is that right? I see, it's for your husband... as you argue a lot.'.......

Patsy:
(On telephone to reception during teatime break in stewards' room)
'You can tell Mr — he might like to 'cuddle *real close*', but we have no double beds, only twins available. He doesn't believe you? Do you want me to come back from tea and tell that to Mr — in person? No, alright, I understand what you're telling me. What now? You're saying Mr Berry is in the foyer and he is motioning...
Yes... hands wafting about, index finger indicating. "No! No! No!" he is saying. Now he is shaking his head from side to side, hiding out of sight, behind a pillar, but what does he mean? I know! Absolutely not, definitely *no* double beds.'

Anne:
'Hello switchboard? Could you put me through to Miss Davies' room please? Thank you. Yes I'll hold.'
'Miss Davies? Good afternoon. I've got your mother here, in reception. Should I send her up? Just a minute. Sorry...? 'No... er... it's .not your mother... it's your sister! '

Stewards' room
Patsy:
'Chef... Chef... Chef-ee! Can we have some salad cream? Can we have some salad cream please? We don't want your mayonnaise?'
Chef:
(Roaring) 'What do you think this is a roadside café?'......

Boss Freely:
(Glasses off and waving them in the air)
'So as you were saying there was an error on your bill sir? Can you remember which bookkeeper served you? They're all dressed in black you know. Yes they are all wearing miniskirts.'

Hotel Guest:
(Leaning, over the desk)
'Yes that one the one with the red knickers with black spots.

Boss Freely:
Speechless, looking blank, thinking, glancing, lost for words, shrugging her shoulders. *Well really. Men.*

Sindy:
'Excuse me, good evening, sir. One moment please, before you leave in the morning could you sign your bill? Many thanks, and could you print the full forwarding address clearly for me?'

Sindy:
'Maureen, who did you say he was?'

Maureen:
'The Governor, Bank of England.'

Sindy:
'No, it wasn't, was it?'

Maureen:
'No... so sorry sir, I can't possibly cash you a cheque. No, not for that amount money. We do have restrictions you know. I don't care who you are or who you know! Yes, I will fetch the manager.'
'Hello, switch board? Can you find Mr Berry? He's needed here, a gentleman in the foyer insists on seeing him, wants to cash a cheque. Won't take no for an answer.'

Hotel Manager:
'Yes that's quite alright sir, the bookkeeper will cash the cheque. Now please... and no... er... Miss Harrison, we don't need the

address on the back…'

Maureen

'Who was that guest? Was that anyone we should know?'

Hotel Manager

'That gentleman was The Queen's equerry, from Buckingham Palace!'

Annie:

(On the fifth floor telephone trying to get connected to the hall porter through the switchboard)

'Hello, Hello? Harry, is that you? It's me on the fifth floor back. There is a football team outside my room. I can't get them to go away. They followed me up here and they don't seem to understand English. I've been waylaid! Can you get hear me Harry!'

CHAPTER TEN
The Spirit Of Place

I

The move to another room, 525A, at the end of the corridor on the fifth floor was given to me as a gesture of goodwill. It was meant to be better because it was a single room, and I suppose I should have been more grateful. Being the second head bookkeeper in the department meant I was the one who opened up in the mornings. You had to be downstairs, in the office, ready and working by six thirty. In a single room I would not disturb anyone.

I reflected it was the first time in my life that I had ever had a room of my own. In some ways it was quite nice to be by myself, but I did not like the room much. It was small, an outside room on a corner where the hotel jutted out, overlooking Copperas Hill and Lime Street Station. The Royal Mail sorting offices and the main milk distribution depot were up the hill and toward the back. In the early morning you could hear the milk bottles rattling in their crates as the milkmen loaded up their floats and started their daily deliveries. The noise signified the start of the day and became part of life.

My lovely big Adelphi window did not open very wide because there was balustrade outside, which made the room seem slightly darker, and there was scaffolding up around the building. This was because the hotel was being cleaned, as were most of the buildings in Liverpool at that time. They were undergoing a facelift to restore them back to their original state. Clean air legislation was making a noticeable difference, and it changed the appearance of the city by getting rid of the horrid black grimy dirt that had become ingrained in the stone buildings for years.

Anyway, I did not care to open the window much as once or twice there had been intruders climbing up the scaffolding onto the ledge outside and the porters had to be fetched to intervene. The hotel porters were general factotums and had to deal with whatever was thrown at them. They would appear out of nowhere to help and assist, and nothing was too much trouble for them. No need for security men.

Then there was noise from the National Express buses as they pulled into the nearby bus station and the tannoy at Lime Street Station. The announcements usually concerned the Pullman service to London Euston. This was especially important for business purposes, because it was a lifeline to the capital city. These Pullman trains were the very latest locomotives for electrified services. They were blue or light grey and looked good, travelling in speeds up to 100 miles per hour. They were much longer trains and had sliding doors, very modern, with better amenities just like the continental trains except for the loos, which weren't much different.

The very last steam train to run went from Liverpool Lime Street Station on 11 August 1968, going to Carlisle and returning to Liverpool for its final journey. Often I could hear the train announcements if the wind blew in the right direction. In fact, the wind simply howled round the corner and blew in great dusty gusts, often coupled with spits of fine rain. As I was hidden away in a lobby, on the end of the corridor I sometimes felt isolated.

Next door to my room lived Pat Freely, the boss. More often than not when Pat finished work she caught the train to Stafford, where her sisters worked for the railway in the refreshment rooms. Occasionally I would knock on Pat's door later on in the evening, to see if she had any milk to make tea, and she would say, 'Come in for a chat, Annie.' Invariably she would be ready for bed with her hair set in rollers, hairpins, and big bulldog clips.

She would have her housecoat on and be busily occupied manicuring and painting her nails. Her transistor radio would be turned on loudly as she listened to her programmes; maybe *Radio Eireann*, *Night Ride*, or *Late Night Extra*. The transistor was held together with an elastic band because it had been dropped so many times. The daily newspaper would be sprawled out on the floor, the crossword half done and she would be writing a letter home; all these things going on at the same time. She was multitasking, but not for long because we needed our rest. Those of us on the morning shift had to be wide awake and on our toes, fully compos mentis.

II

My first breakfast of the day was eaten sitting up in bed. I ate a whole grapefruit at five o'clock in the morning. I peeled it like an orange into segments. With the radio on and the volume turned low I would methodically and systematically begin to get ready for work. Then at five forty-five every single morning the night waiter, an Italian man called Nicki who spoke very little English, brought my early morning tea and toast to the room. He was a man of few words, which was just as well really, given the early hour and that he was difficult to understand.

He would knock on the door and balancing the tea tray would use his pass key. When I heard the tea things rattle I would sometimes jump up and open the door first.

'Good morning, Anna,' he would say and leave the tray on the floor outside, or sometimes he would carry the tray inside the room and deposit it on the coffee table. I looked forward to my tea. Those first few sips worked like magic. The silver tray was beautifully laid complete with two slices of hot buttered toast, cut into fingers ready to eat. Nicki never failed to arrive on time with my tea. You see, it was a vital component to start the day. When it was his rest day the other night waiter would take over. I was never forgotten.

Hotel life worked like that. It ran like clockwork most of the time.

III

The head night porter, Harry, had worked in the hotel since he was a pageboy; now married, he lived up the road with a large number of children, a typical Catholic family. One by one as they grew up they came and worked in the hotel too, a family tradition. Harry was highly esteemed in the hotel. All the old knowledge and traditions from the 'Golden Age' had been passed down to him. He knew it all.

I always felt safe in the hotel at night with Harry on the desk. You could trust him implicitly. He was a sort of custodian of the hotel and seemed to me like a storybook hall porter: gentle, kind, caring, and thoughtful. Harry knew Liverpool like the back of his hand. When the time was right he stepped into Harry Haycock's shoes and became the definitive head hall porter at the Adelphi.

All the hall porters were hardworking, decent men. Some were old, too old to be lifting and carrying heavy suitcases and meeting trains at Lime Street Station in all weathers. On nights they never stopped and would polish shoes, sort and take up the newspapers to the rooms, respond to enquiries from residents, log early morning calls for the night waiter and the night telephonist, Ted. They would tidy up and vacuum the front hall stairs and lounge; help and advise guests attending functions; carry, fetch, and look after the luggage as well as attending the hotel with all its sleepers throughout the night. They worked together and helped each other out long before the phrase 'teamwork' was coined.

The second head night porter was also Harry. The trouble with Harry was that he was such a worrier. He got anxious in case I overslept. Harry gave me an early morning call every single morning at five thirty or thereabouts for years. This would be before the early morning tea arrived. I had to have back up! When you rang down to put the call in with Ted, the night telephonist, he would say if there were many early departures. If it had been a busy night Harry would call out when he knocked.

'Anna, Anna, there is a Cambrian Airline crew checking out first thing. I've got their bills ready.'

Then, 'Anna, Anna, some other guests are leaving early and they want to pay their bill in Deutsche Marks.' I would arrive to find airline pilots and crew all propping up the desk and a group of Germans all waiting to settle their accounts. Harry would be there anxiously waiting for me to emerge from the lift.

If some of the girls were going out for the evening he would say, 'Anna, you're not going out with them?' I never did go out because I was the one who started the ball rolling in the mornings.

IV

Strange happenings sometimes occurred in the hotel. The telephonists knew all about these, but we never paid much attention until one day, upstairs on the fifth floor, a hall porter whom I did not immediately recognise was quietly seen shuffling along the corridor. He did not notice me. This porter looked on the lines of Teddy boy with his hair combed in a quiff and sideboards. He looked tired, stooped as though on his beam end and not quite from this planet. Then he seemed to disappear; he just vanished as if he had been spirited away into one of the nearby bedrooms. I could not see, but it looked like he had been beckoned inside.

He had.

'Would you mind lifting my suitcase on to the portmanteau stool?' said the gentleman in the room. He continued, 'Thank you so much. I could not manage it myself. And if it's not too much trouble,' he went on, 'the window… can't close it properly.'

'Yes, it is chilly in here, sir, like ice,' said the porter, looking round shivering and then spotting a bottle of something,

'Would you like a whisky?' said the guest, catching his gaze.

'Thank you, yes that would be most welcome. I'm new, just started the job this week actually, and I'm full of cold, not at my best. A whisky might be just the ticket to get me through the day,' said the porter.

'Help yourself,' said the gentleman, indicating the half full bottle. The porter poured himself a large scotch and took a mouthful, swilling it round and getting the taste; why, he felt better all ready. When he got to the bottom of his now empty glass he looked up, and in a fleeting moment he saw the gentleman had disappeared. So, the porter thought perhaps he had better hurry up and leave, which he promptly did, calling out, 'I'd best get back now, sir. I'll be off then, and thanks for the drink'. The porter decided the drink must have been in lieu of a tip. Then he saw the covers on the bed had been turned down. How odd he hadn't noticed that before. As he made to leave, the bedroom door blew shut.

'Weird, must be the draught from the window. It's so cold in here. Maybe I shouldn't have had that drink. Oh well, too late, better skedaddle,' he mused.

Downstairs in the hotel foyer the head hall porter was agitated. Where the dickens was the new hall porter? There had been no sign of him anywhere, for ages.

'At last,' said Harry as he saw the porter emerge from the baggage lift. He was relieved more than anything and said, 'Where the heck have you been? We were going to send out a search party!'

'I was helping a gentleman, a resident on the fifth floor, with some things in his room; can't remember the room number, somewhere along the left hand side of the corridor. All I know it was freezing in there.'

'Well, I don't know what you're on about. Those rooms haven't been let for quite a while.' Harry cast his mind back, remembering the incident. 'Not since—' He stopped short.

'What?' asked the porter worried now: 'Not since what?'

Pausing Harry spoke, 'There was a death, a gunshot, a shot in the dark … a suicide. It's never mentioned, a death in the hotel… you know is one of the worst things that can happen. Some say it's haunted up there; people have had a few funny experiences, so to speak,' said Harry coolly, in a matter-of-fact voice.

The porter stared in shock horror. Had he heard correctly? It sounded crazy. Who had he been talking to? Without waiting to find out, he ran like the wind out of the front door and into the Big House the hostelry next door, shaking with fright.

'Steady the buffs, what's up?' said the bartender. 'I'll get you a wee dram. The Adelphi isn't as bad as all that is it? You look like you've seen a ghost!'

And he wasn't far wrong.

V

I had not long occupied my new room when I received a letter from a friend, Christine, who had travelled to Paris with me. She wanted to know if she could come and stay overnight, as she had an early morning flight to catch from Speke Airport.

Christine had stayed with me before when Apollo 8 was launched and set to go to the moon. This was 21 December 1968. Whilst they were in lunar orbit the crew made a Christmas Eve television broadcast, and they read from the book of Genesis in the Bible. It was the most watched television broadcast ever. The space rocket was piloted by James Lovell, the commander was Frank Borman, and the lunar module pilot was William (Bill) Anders, who later stayed in the Adelphi. I have his autograph and we heard first hand about the moon.

Christine was enthralled with the space programme, and we were together again on the night of 20 July 1969 when Neil Armstrong on Apollo 11 landed on the moon. He took his first steps on the moon just after midnight on 21 July. We sat up all night to watch this most historic event on television, although I fell asleep.

Now she was flying out to Canada because she had received a proposal of marriage from a man. A man she didn't know well and whom she had met only a few times with friends but when a telegram from Canada arrived saying, 'Madly in love with you.' Stop. 'Will you marry me?' Stop. 'Paul.'

'Yes,' she replied, 'I love you too.'

And with that she packed her bags and booked her flight and stayed with me for the night at the Adelphi before setting off for her wedding and new life in Canada.

VI

One day when walking through the kitchens a page boy ran up to me and told me one of the kitchen cats had a litter of kittens. So I went to see them. They were adorable, cute, small things and I picked one up to stroke and squeeze. How could I resist it and leave it behind in the kitchen? I couldn't. So hiding the kitten beneath my jacket I took it upstairs to my room to keep; a prisoner.

The kitten sniffed around a bit, exploring. Not content with just looking, she started to climb and jump. Down off the bed, then back up, but climbing was not quite as nice as she expected. She fell on all fours and knocked her nose. I lifted the kitten up onto the windowsill, where she made himself at home and began to clean herself, licking her coat with the tiniest pink tongue.

The helpless thing slept most of the time on the bed, which was incredibly high and must have seemed like Mount Everest. When I was working she could sit on the window sill and look out over Copperas Hill and the Vines public house, better known locally as the Big House. She could watch the draymen unloading barrels of beer. Sometimes the porters would get sent to the pub for change if the cashiers needed it and would stay for a swift half of beer if they were asked, just to be sociable. Kitty would wave her tail about watching all the activity; then there were the pigeons and seagulls to distract her.

Kitty was good company, so sweet and playful, but of course after a short while I was found out. Only my chambermaid had known about it, but she never told. It was the others on the fifth floor who heard her meowing and wanted to play with her. The cat was out of the bag.

It seemed she would have to go back to the basement and earn her living like everyone else in the hotel, by keeping the mouse population down in the kitchen and cellars. There would be other cats for company and she would be happier. I would have to be quick though before Miss Murphy came to ask: 'Are you keeping a cat in your bedroom?'

VI

My chamber maid was called Mary, a softly spoken middle-aged lady with neat iron grey wavy hair and beautiful violet coloured eyes. She worked systematically and quietly as she cleaned. Everyday she made my bed and tidied my room. She gave it an airing and changed the bed, opened the window and brought clean towels.

Having the bed changed everyday was sheer luxury. There used to be a laundry in the hotel, which for years had catered for the ships that docked in the port. All the bed linen, towels, and table linen were exquisitely laundered. The soiled linen from the hotel would be put in the wicker laundry baskets on the floors with the floor number painted on the side. These would be left on the corridors while work was in progress, and then once full were sent down in the back lift to the laundry in the basement. The freshly laundered linen was returned in blue plastic bags.

Every week Mary would give my room a good turn out. She would wipe the windowsills, moving all the accoutrements, then pull out and clean behind the bed, which fitted along the wall lengthways. Next she would clean the skirting board behind the dressing table and buff the mirrors.

The hotel was a structured environment. When it got close to annual leave, Miss Murphy, the head housekeeper, would pay you a visit. She was responsible for the maintenance and upkeep of the rooms, plus the supervision of the chambermaids and cleaners. She informed you that your room would be spring cleaned and redecorated in your absence. It was recommended all ornaments and paraphernalia be tidied away so that surfaces were free and clear. Then Miss Murphy enquired as to what colour you would like the room painted. There was a choice of a few colours: eau de nil, duck egg blue and other soft pastels. I chose the yellow as I thought it would give a sunny cheerfulness to the interior of my room.

Spring cleaning meant a lot of very hard work and involved precision. Everywhere was given a thorough going over, with Miss Murphy on hand to make doubly sure everything was just so and to your liking. As if she hadn't got enough to do. She tried to make life comfortable: maybe a change of armchair, curtain, counterpane, cushions. Everything was repaired, replaced, and returned looking new and fresh.

Miss Murphy treated you on a par with the hotel guests. She didn't drop her standards merely because you were staff. She tried to make your room a desirable place to decamp. The beeswax polish, the smell of newness and fresh paint heightened the sense of place and somewhere to hang your hat. It made returning to work after an absence a more inviting proposition. Her good housekeeping ways of doing things have stayed with me, never to be forgotten, ingrained on the soul.

CHAPTER ELEVEN
Forgetting Things

I

Pat Freely was fifty, a landmark if ever there was one, when she started to have a few funny turns. She felt as though she was keeling over, and the more anxious she became, the more she felt strange and not right. The hotel doctor said it was her age, and she got on with it, but she didn't like this change in the way she felt. It was tiresome. The hotel doctor, the young one this time, wasn't particularly sympathetic, and he didn't seem to go a bundle on women with nerves, and as Pat disliked the doctor business anyway she didn't go again.

Her way of coping with these peculiar feelings was to put on her coat midmorning – this was left on the back of her chair in the front office, ready for the off – and then she would run out of the revolving doors of the hotel as quickly as she could and go shopping out on the town. This retail therapy worked wonders, and she would return an hour or two later as right as rain with a windswept bouffant hairdo and her bargain buys.

We became used to being in the office and running things without her as she left more and more things for us to do, and she was not always 'with it' anyway. As the second in the department, I worked the first shift. The unearthly hours we kept became routine, getting up at what felt like the middle of the night, especially in the thick of winter with those dark rainy mornings and maybe the occasional fall of snow and freezing ice. There would be a definite nip in the air.

As the hotel gradually roused from slumber there was much activity and familiar morning sounds as staff went about their daily business. From the breakfast room the deliciously warming smells of strong tea, freshly ground coffee, and hot toast wafting about was a constant, and all these undisturbed routines and repetitions of hotel life gave us reassurance and a sense of well-being that Pat seemed to have lost.

An early morning tea tray was brought to the front desk at seven o'clock by the night waiter before he went off duty; more tea and hot buttered toast that had to keep us going and revitalize us until breakfast time proper. The little page boys would arrive at reception out of breath, struggling to carry the rather large leather mail bag. It would be crammed full of the day's post, which was heavy, and they would deposit it on the desk. They were warmly clad in their outdoor cloaks, hats, and gloves, having braved the elements.

Pat Freely would arrive on duty at eight o'clock to help cover the breakfasts, and then her main job everyday was the hotel banking. After this she had a million and one other things to do. Sometimes it was overwhelming for her. All the departments came to the desk continually with queries or for change and extra cash if there was special business on in the hotel.

She never had a minute to herself and always had to keep one step ahead of everyone else. The responsibility was enormous. Often fazed with fatigue if she hadn't slept well, there would be a bit of role reversal in our office with us telling her what to do and proffering advice. But as the morning wore on she became more normal, more her old self.

'Imagine,' I said to Maureen, 'getting to that stage in life when your brain just won't function.' We wondered, 'What lies ahead on the other side of fifty?'

Maureen paused for a moment and considered it. 'It doesn't bear thinking about. Anyway, it's a long way off.'

II

On Wednesdays Pat would go through her float, which was massive, and count all the money. This took forever and there was no quick fix. It involved much cursing and swearing, and we sometimes mislaid the big wooden block with the safe key attached. More stress. And so the place would be upside down with all sorts of bits of paper while Pat looked through all her rubbish, which distracted her from the task in hand. It was all rather shambolic. We bookkeepers often felt dishevelled and mucky handling all the bank notes and travellers cheques. The receptionists, on the other hand, were always clean with everything in place and picture perfect, and they got a bit above themselves, or so it seemed from where we were standing.

Pat had to agree a figure, an amount, over the phone with the accountant. The phone lived on the windowsill, and Pat would stand talking to him, looking out through the window, only half listening while she watched the passers-by outside. She loved looking at the larger than life Liverpool characters. Her hand would rest on her hip, and then she would fix her hair with her hands and buff it up at the back while she listened to control.

The head of control was a small, bespectacled man with thick, round glasses with tortoiseshell rims; dark hair slicked back, smart dark suit, and shiny shoes. He had a very 1940s look; a textbook accountant. He referred to everyone as doll.

'Thanks doll,' he would say, peering over his specs. Or, 'Can you find this for me doll?' We all thought of him as old and sexist, so we were very surprised one day when his wife came in the hotel. He had a wife! And she was very pretty, petite, and young!

The other hotel accountant looked more like a man of the cloth with a Friar Tuck hairdo and a ruddy complexion. He had spectacles perched on the end of his nose; it seemed that these were a pre requisite for the job. He said very little, but maybe it was he couldn't get a word in edgeways. Pat was such a tour de force it was sometimes the easier option.

On Thursdays Mr B would descend from control to the front office, and everything had to be just right. Pat would go along with him and his department and make up the hotel wages. It was her job to get the money ready as well; the notes, the silver, and small change to make up the wage packets. It was a long haul, and she would be gone for hours. Sometimes she disappeared into the strong room to count the money in the safe and would return in a lather having forgotten the combination. She would come back to the front office looking as white as a ghost, unable to crack the code, and sit with her head propped in her hands; unable to remember it.

She had lost concentration, her mind gone blank. Pat had completely forgotten it. We did not really understand. Today we would call it a senior moment or maybe a blonde moment. Some might say a Verve Cliquot moment. Whatever, we would be on tenterhooks, willing her to recall the sequence.

'Five turns to the right, four turns to the left, and three to the right, two left, or was it? Is that right, Annie?' And we would get in a muddle. Then she would go through it again and it would go on. I helped Pat as much as possible and Maureen too. We shared our load and made the best of things. Maureen had a keen sense of humour and was a beacon of light, making us laugh at her quips and jokes.

We could not help but glance across toward reception where they would be perched on their high stools with their straight backs, swinging their legs in a flirtatious manner, waiting for the new arrivals to check in; familiar male faces from companies such as McKinsey and Co, Barker and Dobson, or Plessey's, while we were up to our eyes.

III

On my afternoons off I would sometimes saunter along the road to the Central Library, the first lending library in England, with my artist's hat on. I often had an artist revival period. There was always time to draw and mess about even if it was only a doodle. It was on one of these afternoons in the art library I ran into some students I knew. It was a defining point; a sort of seminal moment. Change was around the corner for me, although I didn't know it at the time

I liked their company, the deep debates and lively discussions. It was interesting and different, an intellectual community. I liked joining them on rambles, embracing the great outdoors, walking in the Lake District together. My thoughts became clear. I began to get notions, realising I had missed out on something. I wanted to become a student too. It was time to move on.

It was nice having a social life outside work and the hotel, although it was hard to adjust and resume to a normal life style, surrounded as I was in the hotel by staff that did everything for me, while I did nothing for myself. Re-entry into the wider world might prove more difficult than I'd imagined. Pat didn't know what to think and rallied round, trying to please. She mooted that if Maureen or I considered marrying we should be allowed to keep our jobs. What a novel idea. I suppose she had vision.

Pat worked with good humour. Rolling up her sleeves she went pell mell around the front office helping, but more often than not getting in the way. So we seemed to dash through life at breakneck speed, going from one excitement to another in those days; no time for style. All this was just so we could get through the days business and get a life outside the hotel.

Then unfortunately things took a turn for the worse. Soon after, and not totally unexpectedly, Pat Freely's mother, who was getting on – she was well into her nineties – became ill, and Pat went home to Ireland to be with her. She loved her mother very much. I took on the mantle of head bookkeeper with Maureen now the second in the department.

I missed Pat being around on the fifth floor, as she had the bedroom next to mine. It was too quiet, too lonely. What had happened to everybody? The corridors seemed deserted and the fifth floor empty. I knew that the Irish receptionist on the other side of my room was having a fling with an airline pilot up on the sixth. Every night I would hear the lock in her door click as she proceeded to creep on tiptoe to the back staircase. Then she would furtively run up to join him on the next floor. She never got caught. She was so intensely secretive, but all these nights of love didn't sweeten her or temper her sharp tongue. She could hardly smile.

So I took to sleeping at home quite a lot. Well, occasionally, during the summer months when it was light and warm. I made the effort then. I travelled into work at the crack of dawn by train. Nobody told me not to do this, and I would wear my uniform underneath a duster coat or something similar, going straight to the desk from the railway station.

Maureen would start the first shift on these mornings.

IV

One day I made a decision and I went to see the general manager. I informed him that I wanted to leave my job, my home in the hotel, and go to college. I wanted to train to be an art teacher. He was startled and taken completely aback. It was easy to see he didn't rate teaching as a profession at all and said as much. He thought it a flight of fancy, a whim of mine.

'You realise you're making a mistake.' He studied me evenly for several moments. 'Have you really thought this through carefully?' He deliberated. Was he secretly thinking, 'Another hare-brained idea?' It was written all over his face. Mr B seemed perturbed and unable to grasp my logic, my rationale for wanting to leave the hotel and go into teaching. He just couldn't understand it.

I did not want to listen or hear anymore as my focus had changed. The prospect of studying was alluring, and I had already been to the education offices and made applications. First of all I needed to go to a college of further education and take a couple of A levels and enrol at a school of art. I was not put off or daunted, and I had already taken steps to withdraw my pension to support me as a student along with a small grant.

V

Pat did not come back to work, as I kept hoping, because her mother was hanging on for dear life. It was impossible to let Pat down and just go, leaving friends in the lurch. So I stayed.

September, then October came and went, and still no sign of Pat returning from Ireland. It was getting too late to enrol. The college was understanding but had deadlines. November came and I had to make decisions. Should I wait for the next academic year? I was cutting it fine.

The general manager asked an elderly head bookkeeper from British Transport Hotels to come out of retirement. It took two weeks to hand over and show her how we did things in the Adelphi. Then Maureen organised a huge leaving party, inviting everyone: staff, hotel residents, friends from outside. The 'do' was held in a sixth floor stockroom, and I was presented with a portable typewriter. I vowed to take lessons at Sight and Sound and learn to touch type, which would be useful for writing essays and special studies, and I left the hotel.

Once Pat returned from Ireland, her mother having rallied round this time, she got back into a routine again. I would visit each week on

Tuesdays and have tea with her in the couriers' room. Pat would enjoy making tea for me and looked forward to my visit. We would have fresh boiled eggs, honey, and brown bread and butter, which she would have gone for that morning on one of her shopping sprees out of the office. I was still drawn to the hotel and had an affinity to it. I enjoyed going there each week to visit. It was so familiar welcoming. It was like going back to the mother ship.

VI

I still went there for my tea the following year when I was now at teacher training college. In some ways college life was not much different from the hotel in that I had swapped one institution for another. I was still surrounded by young people from all walks of life and in a residential setting, although some women students were married. Now that was different.

One Tuesday over tea Pat and I were having a tête-à-tête when she broached a special subject. It came out of nowhere.

'I've met a man,' she blurted and carried on pouring tea nonchalantly into my cup, as though it was an everyday occurrence.

'What!' said I, 'A man? What sort of a man?' I was struck dumb. For the first time in my life I temporarily lost the power of speech! This astounding and wholly unexpected news was mind boggling. Starry eyed, excited, Pat spilled the beans, although her feelings went beyond words. She had met someone unique and fallen in love. I listened, incredulous. I thought her days for romance were over, but apparently not.

'Goodness gracious, fallen in love, its unbelievable!' I said scornfully to Maureen afterwards, 'And at her age!'

'Well,' began Maureen in a good natured way, 'wasn't your father fifty-something when he got married for the first time?'

'That was because of the war… It was… different,' I started to exclaim, but I had no real answer. And we left it at that.

Pat didn't know if she was coming or going, on her head or her heels. They were mad for each other. Ed, her intended, was ten years older again. I thought him old. At sixty-four he was rather well stricken in years.

'He's a scientist, little Annie,' Pat said proudly, 'and extremely clever. He's an engineer at Rolls Royce. He pioneered the air conditioning in Roll Royce cars in the 1930s and drove around America in the cars. His brother worked with Sir Henry.'

'Great,' said I, but all the time I was really thinking of myself.

Pat had known Ed when she was young and now later in life he was a widower and available. I wondered if they remembered what they had felt before. I was sure they did, even though so many years had passed since they had first met.

Eddie owned a Bentley, which he changed for a smaller, different car, a mini, because at this point Pat was still learning to drive; still learning after all these years. She practised her driving in the mini. One day when out with them in the car, with Ed acting as an instructor, he watched Pat as she climbed out of the driver's seat and without thinking linked arms with me and together we walked away, busily chattering, in a world of our own.

'Pat dear,' called Ed, and when Pat turned around, still talking nineteen to the dozen, she scarcely noticed at first she had left the car engine running and the car door wide open. So after that she decided to call it a day. 'No more driving Dwarling.'

Eddie could drive instead and she would marry him. And that's what happened.

VII

It was one of those whirlwind romances and the banns went up in the Liverpool Metropolitan Cathedral of Christ the King. Pat and Ed celebrated their engagement and forthcoming marriage by holding a candlelit dinner party at the Port Hole Restaurant in Bold Street. We all dressed up in our finery, wearing the poshest of frocks and stayed overnight as guests in the hotel. There was much to celebrate. Pat had that glow about her that only comes with being in love, even at her great age and after the first flush of romance.

Ed was indeed so fortunate to have won the heart of such a good woman. It was wedding bells soon afterwards, and the change in her was truly amazing. There's nothing like being in love to make women radiant and lit up.

A magical transformation had taken place; Pat accepted this happiness and took it with open arms. Marriage had happened to Pat, and how easily she adapted to this change in her life.

So, that part of the story is done with, finished. It was the end of an era. Our salad days were gone forever, but we had had the best of times. We'd had the time of our lives.

It was on this idyllic high note Pat took her departure and left the hotel.

EPILOGUE

Recollections of the Adelphi Hotel remain vivid even after many years. However, a selective memory can distort things until myth and reality merge into one, and accuracy depends on how things are perceived at the time. The reader may see flaws in my reminiscences because it all happened such a long while ago. History is not what you thought, but what you remember.

There isn't an end to the story as such either. The hotel stayed in sight for another decade while it remained part of British Transport Hotels.

Maureen, who figured so prominently in the latter half of my working life in the hotel, became the head bookkeeper after Pat left. She then moved to greener pastures at the London Ritz Hotel and from there, the Southampton Princess Hotel, Hamilton, Bermuda, where she lived for many, many years before settling in Florida, marrying, and having two wonderful children.

Jeanette, who married Keith – aka Frank Sinatra – an assistant manager, moved to her home ground with her husband in Newcastle. She is still a bluestocking, and they have a lovely son.

Pat became an adored Granny Pat to my children and took part in high days and holy days along with all the Irish sisters and Eddie. They made it to twenty-five years married, just.

Olwen Davies never married, although she had her moments. She became part of our home and family and a very much loved Aunty Olwen to Rose and Emily, Esme and Anna. After leaving the hotel she took a flat in Rodney Street; where else! She stayed a stylish, sophisticated, and sparkling lady all her life.

Lucinda spent a great many years living abroad and much time travelling and exploring. She remained a kind and generous friend and has five gorgeous boys.

She still eats Brazil nuts.

Staff List

General Manager
Assistant Managers
Banqueting Manager
Staff Manager
Marketing and Sales Manager
Trainee Managers

Secretary
Junior Secretaries

Reception manager
Shift Leaders
Receptionists

Head Bookkeeper
2nd Head Bookkeeper
Bookkeepers

Theatre Bookings

Cloakroom Attendant (female)

Head Telephonists
Telephonists
Night telephonist

Head Porter
Second Head Porter
Day Porters
Porter- Cloakroom Attendant (male) / Newspapers

Head Night Porter
Second Night Porter
Night Porters

Car Jockey
Garage Attendant
Page boys'

Barber

Lounge Staff
Head Waitress
Lounge Waiters
Night Waiters

Floor Waiters
Waiters

Head Housekeeper
Second Head Housekeeper
Housekeepers

Plumbers

Electricians

Engineer

Locksmith

Valets

Painter

Sewing Room Ladies

American Bar
Head Barman/ Manager
Second Head Cocktail Barman
Bar Staff

Restaurant Manager French
Maitre D'
Restaurant Cashiers
French Wine Office
Wine Waiters
Waiters
Floor Waiters
Pianist

Sefton Grill Manager
Restaurant Cashier
Head Wine Waiter
Head Waiter
Head Cellar Man
Waiters

Kitchen Clerk
Stores
Lift Man
Kitchen Porter
Kitchen Staff
Dishwashers
Glass Washers
Silver Cleaner/Cutlery Cleaner

Head Chef
Chef
Bakers and Confectioners
Pastry Chef
Chef
Commis Chef
Chef de Partie
Sous Chef
Plate Man
Casuals

Head Waiter
Second Banqueting Waiter
Head Banqueting Waiter
Head Banqueting Porter
Extra Waitresses

Printer
Painter and decorator
Pig Swill Man

Staff/Games Room
Stewards' room Staff
Courier Room Staff
Still Room Staff

Head of Staff Office
Office Staff
Accountant

Head of Control
Second Head
Control Staff
Ledger Clerk

House Detective

END NOTES

Prologue

1) The Adelphi Hotel on the present site was opened in 1826 by James Radley.
2) In 1912, Arthur Towle rebuilt it. Frank Atkinson, who married into the Towle family, designed the interior circa 1914. It was not completed. This was just before the First World War.
3) Graham Green described the Adelphi as having 'the right ideas about comfort and a genuine idea of magnificence.'
4) The Maitre D' (Maitre D'Hotel) assigns guests to their tables and divides the restaurant into areas of responsibility for the waiters on duty. He was responsible for reservations for dining and discussing the menu with the chef.
5) The railways were nationalised on 1 January 1948. In 1963 British Transport Hotels were formed into a subsidiary company, and ownership passed onto British Railways Board. BTH sold off the hotels piecemeal, between 1981 and 1983. The company owned approximately thirty five hotels, plus the refreshment rooms up and down the country:

York, Royal York Hotel
West Hartlepool, Grand Hotel
Sutherland, Dornoch Hotel
Stratford, Welcombe Hotel, Warwickshire
Sheffield, Royal Victoria Hotel
Saltburn by the Sea, Zetland Hotel
Peterborough, Great Northern Hotel
Perthshire, Gleneagles Hotel
Perth, Station Hotel
Newcastle, Royal Station Hotel
Morecombe, Midland Hotel
Manchester, Midland Hotel
Liverpool: Adelphi Hotel and the Exchange Hotel
Leeds, Queens Hotel
London: Great Western, Paddington, Great Northern, Kings Cross,
Great Eastern, Liverpool Street, and Charing Cross Hotels
Kyle of Lochalsh, Lochalsh Hotel, Ross-shire

Inverness, Station Hotel
Hull, Royal Station Hotel
Glasgow: St Enoch Hotel, North British Hotel, and Central Hotel
Edinburgh: Caledonian Hotel, Princes Street and
North British Hotel, Waverly Station
Aberdeen, Station Hotel
Ayrshire, Turnberry Hotel
Birmingham, Queens Hotel
Bradford, Midland Hotel
Cornwall, Tregenna Castle, St Ives
Derby, Midland Hotel
Devon, Manor House, MoretonHampsted
Dumfries, Station Hotel

6) Nicholas Monserrat's father was a surgeon. The great Victorian Premier, William Gladstone, was born at 62 Rodney Street. Doctor Duncan, the first Public Officer of Health, lived at number 54, and Lytton Strachey, the writer and biographer, at number 80 Rodney Street.

7) Alan Durband, an important figure in education and the arts, was co-founder of the Everyman Theatre and his 'English Workshop' text book was used in many secondary schools in Liverpool in the 1960's

Chapter 1: Fifth Floor Convent

1) Tights and stockings: mid-1960 brought huge changes: Aristoc and Wolford were at the forefront. In 1967 tights became an innovation and Aristoc started production. In 1969 Wolford established a link with Dupont and used a thread called Cantrice, which gave elasticity and stretch. In 1975 ladder-proof hosiery was developed. Young miniskirt wearers bought tights; corsets and girdles were discarded.

Chapter 2: The Bed Sitting Room

1) The 1960s was turbulent decade: the war in Vietnam, social unrest, campaign for nuclear disarmament, and opposition to nuclear power stations.
2) 21 August1968 England defeated Australia at the Oval in the final test to draw the Ashes series: D'Oliveira 158/Graveney 63. The Aussies took the Ashes home.
3) At Wimbledon 1968, Rod Laver beat Tony Roche and Billy Jean King beat Judy Tegart.
4) The Art College was on the corner of Hope Street and had its origins as part of the Liverpool Institute for Boys circa 1883.
5) Liverpool Institute Blackburne House for Girls was on the opposite side of the street.
6) The Art College was itself an institution and accepted students on merit with portfolio. In 1970 it became part of Liverpool Polytechnic.
7) James Harold Wilson, Prime Minister KG OBE FRS PC (1916–1995). Served as prime minister, first term from 1964–70 and second term 1974–76. Harold Wilson did much to increase opportunities for people by changing the education system. He introduced the concept of the Open University. He brought in the Divorce Reform Act, abolished capital punishment, and changed the law on homosexual issues.
8) He made many changes in social areas.
9) "Hey Jude" was a hit for The Beatles, reaching no 1 on 28 September 1968. It played for seven minutes.
10) The Beatles *White Album* was released 22 November 1968.

Chapter 3: The Time We Got Drunk on Success

1) Margaret Kelly founded the Bluebell Girls. She directed the dances at the Folies Bergere in Paris. The girls had to possess certain

qualities: beauty, poise, and grooming.

2) They had to be long legged and tall. They were mostly ballet trained and their costumes were spectacular. They wore stiletto heels, which gave them extra height. They were a celebrated and prestigious dancing troupe.

3) Scottish black tie. The dress code here included a dirk, dress sporran, skean dubh, kilt hose (monogrammed), black ghillie brogues or black dress shoes, white shirt, black waistcoat, black jacket, kilt.

4) The writer likens the Adelphi to Buckingam Palace. The Palace is built in Portland stone, which is quarried on the Isle of Portland, Dorset. It has been used throughout Britain in major public places, such as St Paul's Cathedral and the Cenotaph in Whitehall, and the United Nations building in New York. It was also used for the many gravestones for British personnel after the Second World War.

5) The very lovely Adelphi windows were set in smooth Portland stone with beautiful decorative carving by H.H. Martyn & Co.

6) The Anglican cathedral built on St James' Mount has the heaviest ring of bells, and the bells in Liverpool Metropolitan Cathedral are called Matthew, Mark, Luke, and John.

Chapter 4: No Angels

1) C.S. Lewis: from 'A Grief Observed.'

Chapter 5: Boss Freely

1) The contraceptive pill was available to married women from 1961. It was developed by an American biologist and it worked by suppressing ovulation.

2) The take up of the pill between 1962 and 1969 was fifty thousand to over one million women. It was not available to single women

until 1967. After the Second World War and toward the end of the 1940s, over nine hundred thousand babies were born, and they became known as the Baby Boom generation.

3) Margaret, my sister, was a midwife on the district in Toxteth. She delivered many of the babies born into Liverpool families who were employed in the hotel.

4) Rosemary, eldest sister and a Blackburne house girl, was a primary school teacher in Windsor Street for a while, and she taught children belonging to the hotel staff.

5) Harold Wilson and the Labour government in the 1960s saw a time of unrest, unemployment, and a series of strikes (1969).

6) We missed many an exciting opportunity… of being picked up. Pat saw her role as in 'loco parentis'. She had a great respect for my father who had been a soldier in the First World War: on the Somme, then in the Easter Risings in Ireland, and as a guide in the Balkans. During the Second World War he was home guard. It was in his role as a shop keeper in Everton that he was best known amongst the Adelphi staff: for his kindness and generosity during lean post war years, when money rarely changed hands and food bills were put 'on a tab'.

Chapter 6: Jules Misbehaves

1) Black tie dress code was used for formal events. The black coat and dinner jacket worn goes back to 1860. It was a short coat made of wool or mohair, ventless, with silk facings, usually single breasted.

2) The trousers had no turn-ups and had matching silk braids. The waist was dressed with a black cummerbund and white cotton or linen shirts with matching gold or silver studs and cufflinks.

3) The black silk bow tie could be woven grain or satin finish and either butterfly shape (tall) or batwing (thin), but definitely not pre-tied!

4) Shoes were either patent leather or highly polished, maybe black leather oxford lace ups with a rounded toe with knee-high silk socks.

5) The first Lamborghini was introduced in 1964 by an Italian called Ferruccio. The Lamborghini Espada was made between 1968 and 1978. It was designed by Marcello Gandini. Espada means 'sword' in Spanish. Three different models of the car were made, and it was a great success.

Chapter 7: Paris is Divine

1) May 1968, Paris: Riots. Student protests and general strike throughout.
2) France: Focus on education and employment. The strikes had a big social impact.

Chapter 8: A Special Occasion

1) The Grand National. First run in 1839 under the title, The Grand Liverpool Steeplechase. It took up its present title in 1847. The race is run over four-and-a-half miles at Aintree, with thirty fences to jump.
2) The kitchen was run on the brigade system. The title, 'chef' is the abbreviated form of the French chef de cuisine, meaning head of kitchen. Training to be a chef took about four years, starting off with first year commis, second year commis chef, and so on.
3) They worked in sections of the kitchen, such as the starter/entrée section or vegetable section, under the chef de partie. The chef de partie was the line cook or station chef, of which there were several. Station chef titles included sauté chef; sauces were the highest rank.
4) There was a fish chef (fish butchering), roast chef, grill chef, vegetable chef; a rounds man or swing chef, pantry chef, and pastry chef; pastry was a different team .The sous chef was under chef of kitchen and second in command. He was responsible for scheduling, timetables, covering off duty, and assisting the chef de

partie.

5) The expediter took orders from the dining room and relayed them to the stations in the kitchen.

6) The dishwasher was the keeper of the dishes, in charge of the dishes and keeping the area clean. The kitchen porter usually worked in the kitchens, helping out and assisting. There was no formal training needed.

7) A commis is an apprentice that works under the chef de partie to learn the stations' rules and operation. The chef's uniform dates to the sixteenth century. The uniform included a toque.

8) The toque was tall to allow air to circulate above the head and also allow air to permit outlet of heat. The different height of the chef's hat denoted rank within the kitchen. The symbolism of the folds represents the 100 ways chef knows how to cook an egg.

9) The white double-breasted jacket is made so it can be reversed to hide stains and splashes. The thick cotton protects from the oven's heat and also protects from spittings of boiling liquid. White repels the heat and also denotes cleanliness.

10) Cloth buttons were used because they could stand up to frequent hot washes and they did not melt. The houndstooth pattern on the trousers served to camouflage stains. The necktie was originally worn to allow for mopping the brow. Steel-toe or plastic-capped shoes or clogs were worn to prevent injury from falling sharp implements.

11) Long aprons were worn below the knee to assist in the prevention of accidents and burns.

Chapter 9: Behind the Scenes on Reception

1) We met so many interesting and remarkable people.

Chapter 10: The Spirit of Place

1) Apollo 8, 21–27 December 1968. This marked the first time man orbited the moon. The far side of the moon was seen and planet Earth as a whole. The command module pilot was Jim Lovell. On Christmas Eve they broadcast live and the crew read from the book of Genesis.

2) William Anders began, 'In the beginning God created heaven and the earth and the earth was without form and void and darkness was on the face of the deep.'

3) Jim Lovell read, 'And God called the light Day and the darkness he called Night. And the evening and the morning were the first day.'

4) Borman ended, 'And God said let the waters under the heavens be gathered together unto one place and let the dry land appear; and it was so.'

5) 11 August 1968 ended the passenger steam travel. Stanvier 5 black locomotive 45110 from Carlisle to Liverpool marked the last trip (120mls). Fred Smith from Old Swan was the driver and Stephen Roberts of Kirby the fireman. The train travelled via Manchester Victoria at 7.58 PM.

6) Clean Air Act 1968 was enforced to improve the health of the nation and extend the average age and lifespan.

Chapter 11: Forgetting Things

1) Rolls Royce Partnership between Charles Stewart Rolls and Frederick Henry Royce (Rolls Royce Ltd) 1906. First cars had ten horsepower, two-cylinder engines, and angled radiators, for which the cars are well known, and they had a big following with nobility. Crewe factory opened 1938.

2) According to *Pears* encyclopaedia, the menopause has no influence whatever on sexual life. It is recounted that on being asked by

Voltaire when a woman ceased to feel desire, a famous courtesan at the age of eighty replied, 'I don't know. I haven't lived long enough.'

ILLUSTRATIONS

ADELPHI HOTEL
RANELAGH PLACE
LIVERPOOL, 1

A British Transport Hotel

Telex: 62644

Telephone: ROYAL 7200
Telegrams: TRANSOTEL. LIVERPOOL

PRIVATE BOX NO. 16

LSD:JP:

12th June, 1968.

Miss C. Anne Heald,
19 Roskell Road,
Hunts Cross,
LIVERPOOL. 25.

Dear Madam,

Thank you for your letter of 5th June, from which
I am pleased to learn that you have accepted the position
of Book-keeper/Receptionist at this Hotel.

I should be pleased if you could arrive at the Hotel
during the evening of Sunday, 23rd June, in order to commence
duty on Monday, 24th June, 1968. Your commencing rate of
pay will be 124/6d. per week, plus 12/6d. service charge,
living-in with all meals. When on duty it is necessary to
wear a black dress with long sleeves.

On arriving at the Hotel please ask to see the duty
Assistant Manager.

Yours truly,

H. A. BERRY,
Manager.

FORTHCOMING ATTRACTIONS

16th September
AUDREY JEANS

7th October
THE BEVERLEY SISTERS

21st October
RONNIE DUKES & RICKY LEE

4th November
MICHAEL BENTINE

11th November
DAVID & MARIAN DALMOUR

Shakespeare Cabaret Theatre

□

FRASER STREET, LIVERPOOL

Telephone 207 2278

5.

ARTISTES BOOKED TO APPEAR AT THE SHAKESPEARE THEATRE

Week commencing 15th July

THE KING BROTHERS
THE SAINTS SHOWBAND
ROY DOUGLAS
RICKY GERMAINE

Week commencing 22nd July

EARLE & VAUGHAN
THE GO LUCKY FOUR
TIM LANE
SHEILA & SANDRA

Week commencing 29th July

JOHNNY DUNCAN & THE BLUE
GRASS BOYS
BAL MOANE
MIC & MAC EYNER
SHIRLEY DAVIS
THE 3 HARMANIACS

Week commencing 5th August

THE STATESMEN WITH TERRY
WEBSTER
THE LORNE GIBSON TRIO
VICTOR SEAFORTH
PAULA DARRELL

Week commencing 12th August

THE DEEP RIVER BOYS
THE DARRELL SISTERS
PAUL KELLEY
ROBERTA & HELLA

Week commencing 19th August

BILLY FURY
THE VOYAGERS
TONY FORD
KATHY MARTIN

Week commencing 26th August

THE GIBSONS
THE LAURELS
JOHNNY MOORE

Week commencing 2nd September

WAYNE FONTANA
THE LINACRES
JACKIE IRELAND
MAXINE BARRY

Week commencing 9th September

RAY FELL
THE RAG DOLLS
AL TORINO
THE CONNOISSEURS

A Room in the Town

**ADELPHI HOTEL
RANELAGH PLACE
LIVERPOOL, 1**

Telephone 051 709 7200
Telegrams TRANSOTEL. LIVERPOOL
PRIVATE BOX NO. 56

A British Transport Hotel
Telex: 62644

JP:

23rd October, 1968.

Miss C.A. Heald,
19 Roskell Road,
Hunts Cross,
LIVERPOOL. 25.

Dear Miss Heald,

I was extremely sorry to learn of the sudden death of your mother, and would like to offer my sincere condolences in your sad bereavement.

Thank you for forwarding your medical certificate, which is returned herewith. After completing and signing this form please forward same to your local office of the Ministry of Social Security in order that sickness benefit can be paid.

With compliments,

Yours sincerely,

H. A. BERRY,
Manager.

Please address your reply to the Manager and quote Reference

241

Berlin — Hauptstadt der DDR
Берлин — столица ГДР
1. Bode-Museum
2. Nationalgalerie
3. Pergamonmuseum
4. Museum für Deutsche Geschichte

Verlag Felix Setecki, Berlin

Miss Anne Heald
19 Roskell Road
Hunts Cross
LIVERPOOL
ENGLAND.

East Berlin. Monday.

Dear Anne,
Today i visit E. Berlin it was rather frightening crossing the border & it took about forty minutes for us to be allowed through. the standard of living here is not so high as in the West naturally. Having a fantastic time have French love X.

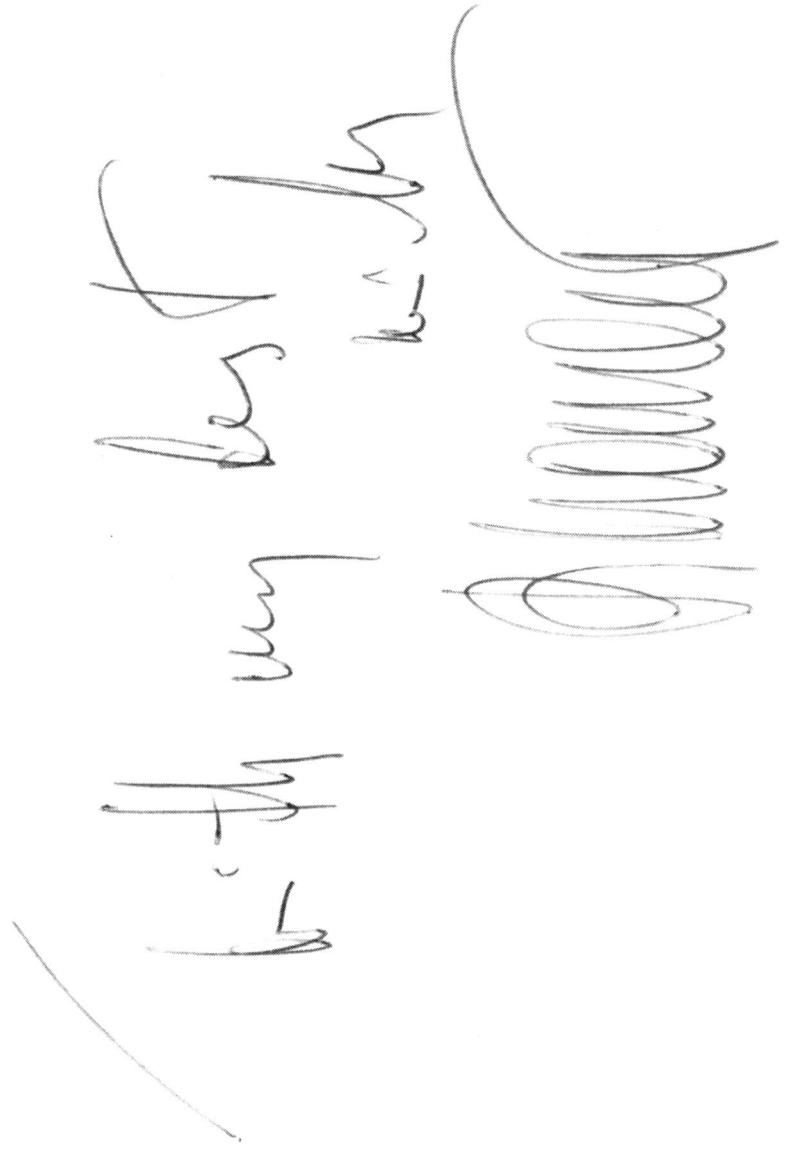

LE DEJEUNER

~

Potage Villageoise 30p

~

Carbonnade de Bœuf Flamande £1 . 50

Gigot d'Agneau Rôti,
                Sauce Menthe ...... £1 . 50

~

The prices of all main dishes
includes vegetables

~

Entremets de la Voiture 30p

Le Plâteau de Fromage...... .... 30p

Douvre Sole	....	£1 . 90
Homard	....	£3 . 00

16th. February, 1972

245

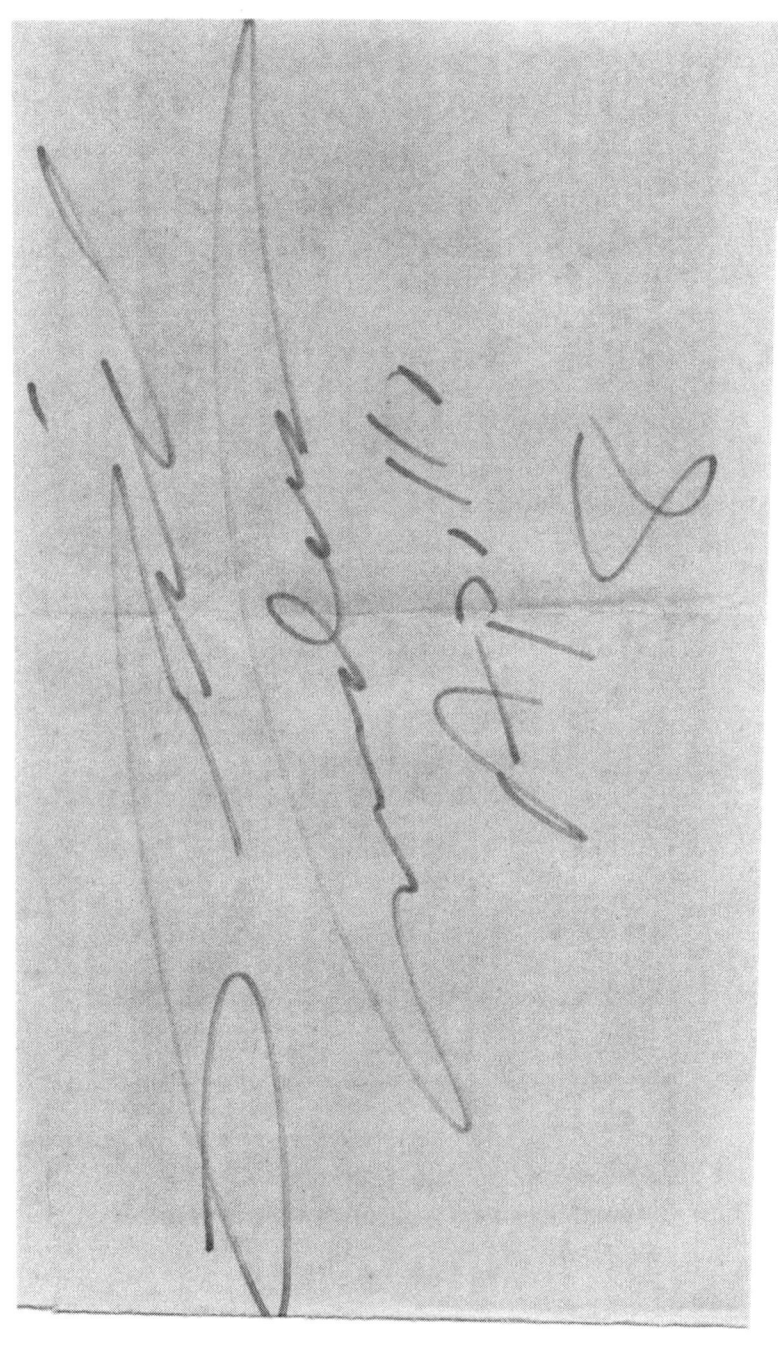

adelphi —
30/7/72

My dear Anne,

Thanks for your letter. Sorry I have not written before this but as you can imagine I don't know if I am going or coming.

Having a little dinner party on Fri. 3rd. So will expect you around 7.15 pm. Going for a drink somewhere first then on to the 'port hole'. Mr Di Marco has arranged the

°/ meal so it should be
good. well you + my
Mannen or I later in the week
as some of the girls want
to wear long frocks. — ??

By the way Mannen said
She had mentioned the 'do'
to you, so hope you have
Kept 3rd. free —
all news when I see you
fondest love pd.

Anne Heald

Anne Heald was a student at St Helens College of Technology and the Gamble Institute, School of Art. She studied at St Katharine's Teacher Training College, taking art and design as her main subject, and the University of Liverpool, where she read Special Education. She has taught in Cheshire schools and was a college lecturer in further education. Before embarking on teaching as a career she was employed for five years by British Transport Hotels at the Adelphi Hotel Liverpool.

Printed in the United Kingdom by
Lightning Source UK Ltd., Milton Keynes
140533UK00002B/1/P